TAO of Survival
Spirituality in social care and counselling

David Brandon

VENTURE PRESS

BASW website: http://www.basw.co.uk

Published by
VENTURE PRESS
16 Kent Street
Birmingham
B5 6RD

British Library Cataloguing-in-Publication Data
A catalogue record for this book is available from the British Library

ISBN   1 86178 048 6 (paperback)

Cover design by:
Western Arts
194 Goswell Road
London
EC1V 7DT

Printed in Great Britain

Contents

Page

Preface

A very long quarter of a century ago, I wrote the book *Zen in the Art of Helping* as a relatively young social worker who had recently turned into an academic. Hopefully it was a light and gentle protest against the dullness and inorganic nature of most of the contemporary social work and counselling textbooks. Very little has changed. The books still take themselves extremely seriously. The helping professions reflect hardly anything of the fragile excitements and dynamic fears of everyday practice. Our teaching rarely catches the flight of the bumblebee, rather it flattens it between academic bricks.

This new book is also written as an antidote to those textbooks. They are usually the products of *Yang* and this comes from *Yin*. Yang is associated with form, order, systems, shape and structures. Yin is linked with opening out, availability, flexibility, malleability and acceptance. Yin is often seen as passive; yang as active. The relationship between these two related elements is highly important in health and social services.

I am now coming towards the end of my career (but am not yet there). This particular work is written in a similar vein to the Zen book. I have been in so many different professions: nursing, administration, academia, social work, priesthood, psychotherapy, journalism and broadcasting and of course my first and last love – writing. I have remained highly sceptical of all of them. Bernard Shaw's words 'All professions are conspiracies against the laity' have rung always in my ears. (*The Doctors Dilemma*, 1906, Act 1).

In many ways the challenge is even greater than it was all those years ago. We think we know much more. We've become a great deal more materialistic. We've developed an aridly technical language to explain away distress and vulnerability and become technicians, moving from the shamanic traditions. We've rejected direct terms such as poverty and battering and replaced them with hateful euphemisms such as 'disadvantaged'; and I, once simply a 'battered child', have become a 'victim of non-accidental injury'. I feel more like a doughty and difficult survivor.

This book contains no considered argument in favour of particular theoretical positions. It even argues with itself. My views are constantly changing. As well as teaching and training over the last few decades, I have also been a practitioner and so know a little of how complicated the issues of supporting distressed and poverty stricken people are. I have become even more sceptical about our reasons for helping. There is a very fine line between intervention and interference. Many support methods are fundamentally injurious to both professionals and their clients. I have scattered a great deal of material from the hindering themes that first appeared in the Zen book

So what follows is an untidy mixture of autobiography, especially from my own social work and counselling experiences; quotations, mostly from oriental sources that may be unfamiliar; and lots of other stories that hit hard on the relevant nails. Stories contain the essence of what we do. I agree joyfully with Gregory Bateson, of whom Capra wrote: 'he considered stories, parables and metaphors to be essential expressions of human thinking, of the human mind. Although he was a very abstract thinker, he would never deal with any idea in a purely abstract way but would always present it concretely by telling a story.' He defined stories as 'an aggregate of internal relations scattered in time.' (Capra, 1988 pp 80–1)

Throughout I've sprinkled Taoist quotations all over the place, with their earthy humour and directness, spiced with some serious Zen irreverence. I have used the *Tao Te Ching* especially, my regular reading and guide over many years. Although more than two millennia old, it has a freshness and vitality that still readily applies to our survival.

I'm not a master of anything but a beginner in over a dozen different areas. Twenty years ago I was ordained a Zen Buddhist monk. I've been a gypsy far too long, never settling in one place. I'm definitely not an expert in life, except in the terms that an old friend of mine is. He's been married disastrously three times and runs marital workshops. He responded to one sarcastic query about his competence – 'If I'm not an expert then who is?' Although I've only been married once – and I'm still living with the same woman, Althea – I understand fully this use of the term 'expert'.

I've made too many major misjudgements to pretend to many skills or much learning. The world is chock full of people who would bear fervent witness to my persistent and consistent stupidity. I write from the deep mud in the valley, not from some high spiritual mountain summit. My life is just an ordinary mess, buffeted about by the winds of lust and desires, an ignoble struggle against sometimes almost overwhelming odds. I've tried to develop some discipline through long years of meditation and regular running. It hasn't come easy. Hopefully you will find something here that matches your experiences of surviving and perhaps even helps. I want to honour our intentions as well as note our failings. I hope that you are challenged by and also enjoy what is contained in these pages.

Some parts of *TAO of Survival* have appeared elsewhere. In particular – a version of chapter 2 was published in CHANGES – an international Journal of Psychology and Psychotherapy Volume 1, No 4, 1996 and a version of the material about my father-in-law in Chapter 6 appeared in Chapter 13 of *Mental Health Care for Elderly People,* Ian Norman and Sally Redfern (Eds.), Churchill Livingstone, 1997.

I thank the many who have contributed to this book. I value greatly the support of my friend Professor Shula Ramon; the laughter of Dr Woody Caan; the essential probings of various Zen teachers, both here and in the United States; the profound contributions and encouragement of my young social work colleagues Lana Morris and Rea Maglajlic; the contributions of some former colleagues at Anglia Polytechnic University; my old friend Kay Carmichael continues to provide a flood of disturbing and usually totally unanswerable questions; my two sons Stewart and Toby are a continual source of surprise and mostly pleasure. My greatest inspiration comes as always from my wife Althea, who is a constant source of surprise, love and wisdom, as well as just putting up with my extremely tiresome stupidities over the last 40 years. I hope this strange book is some small repayment to them all.

David Brandon
Scarborough
North Yorkshire
David.Brandon@tesco.net

Chapter 1
Pointing the Finger

When a wise man points a finger at the moon, a fool looks at the finger.
(Old Zen saying).

This introduction outlines the main themes of the book and then briefly describes the contents of the following chapters. The sardonic Zen saying about pointing the finger captures the truth, that a good teacher points in the right direction but the student stares just at the finger. Speaking from my own stupidity as a student, I know the great truth of that. We need to see far beyond our narrow and partial concerns and pay attention to the Tao and wider compassion, but a good spiritual teacher is always like an alarm clock who wakes himself up whilst the student sleeps on.

Problems and solutions
Our contemporary society is beset with a huge variety of social, economic and spiritual 'problems'. We are increasingly anxious and develop an ever-widening range of solutions – from psychotherapeutic to pharmaceutical, from relaxation to meditation, from yoga to biofeedback. We seek various certainties. Assorted gurus, from the mainstream to the flaky, pronounce on all possible and impossible ways to attain some utopian fragments in every magazine, journal, newspaper, radio and TV station. Most offer rainbow dogmas, try to convince us that we need their special skills and know-how. In their eyes we are usually lesser people – defective or traumatised, who need mending and healing. Such gurus usually appreciate both lots of cash and worship. Given thousands of dollars we could become like them, as the evangelism of their books, tapes, CDs and nowadays websites announces.

Smail, a prominent dissident psychotherapist, writes:

> *'It is extremely difficult to think of any major text in these fields which does not either belittle those who become the objects of its attention, or patronise them by holding before them an ideal of how they ought to be. At the same time, there is of course, absolutely nothing to justify such professional conceit – no evidence that the authors of such texts know better than anyone else how to live their lives, and none that the application of their methods actually leads to a significant amelioration of distress.'* (Smail, 1993 p. 193)

But this wise insight does nothing to halt the personal growth juggernaut, the lust for designer personalities and souls. Popular spiritual books featuring

1

angels, miracles and even chicken soup are carried away from bookshops by the barrow-load.

This disparagement is not accidental. These professionals trade on making us feel mildly to severely inadequate, as with much contemporary advertising. 'Buy this book/cassette tape and you'll be a better parent.' 'Use our new product and you'll look like a million dollars.' 'Make the sheets shine with brilliant new Washo and be a better Mum.' They exploit our negative feelings about ourselves so we feel even flabbier – physically, psychologically and spiritually. They promote the immense and highly profitable illusion that we can improve by purchasing their products.

Pop psychology is a huge growth industry. 'The therapists transformed age-old human dilemmas into psychological problems and claimed that they (and they alone) had the treatment. . . . The result was an explosion of inadequacy' (Sykes, quoted in Dineen, 1996, p. 33) Daytime TV is packed full of programmes where distressed people crowd into studios to disclose their innermost secrets and bizarre doings and get fifteen minutes of fame. The captions underneath the exposed faces scream: 'MARRIED WOMAN KILLS BOTH CHILDREN WITH AN AXE.' 'TRANSEXUAL STRIPPER REVEALS ALL.' 'GAY PRIEST HAD SEX ON ALTAR.'

People almost beg to expose their intimate pain and suffering, mostly great anger and rage at how other people have misbehaved towards them. The world is negatively different from how they had always imagined it. They receive from their TV hostess and the assorted studio counsellors and psychologists, small capsules of 'wisdom', mostly various versions of 'Take more control of your life.' Every time they exercise personal power, the audience claps and stamps its feet. The big message is 'Show life who the Boss is'. When lost in a forest, as in life, just run faster.

Stress has become the biggest reason for time off work, beating the common cold or flu. We find it much harder to survive, simply to cope. We fall short of ever-increasing demands from many different sources. Some ruthless goddess keeps putting up the high jump bar. We should – ought to, have got to – analyse our thousands of personal inadequacies. Each day we discover more. We've grown up in a culture of continually examining ourselves, of self-conscious living. We are not just contemplating the navel but also the toes, fingers and other intimate parts. We are self-conscious and striving citizens, parents and even lovers, judging by the sale of sex instruction books. Perhaps we should practise jumping underneath the bar, rather than over it?

Working on ourselves

Most of us are currently'working on ourselves', trying to become better versions of who we think we are. It even infects popular TV soap operas such as *EastEnders* and *Coronation Street*. The phrase 'working on yourself' conveys a cartoon of a boiler-suited man working underneath himself with hammers and spanners. We buy and read enormous quantities of glossy personal growth books, queue for self-improvement tapes, and increasingly pay to visit a horde of therapists and counsellors. We rely on the insights of strangers. Ours has become a culture of extreme introspection and reflection, like living in a Woody Allen film. We live increasingly intentionally, unlike our parents and grandparents, who wrestled with two world wars, in which the flower (the male flower at least) of a generation died in the stinking Somme mud. We try to increase our options and estimate every conceivable consequence. Fun and spontaneity are reserved for the annual fortnight holiday in Benidorm, Ibiza or river rafting along the Amazon.

The profound horrors of this are conveyed by Roethke (1986):

> *Self-contemplation is a curse*
> *That makes an old confusion worse.*
> *Recumbency is unrefined*
> *And leads to errors in the mind.*
> *Long gazing at the ceiling will*
> *In time induce a mental ill.*
> *The mirror tells some, but not*
> *Enough to merit constant thought.*
> *He who himself begins to loathe*
> *Grows sick in flesh and spirit both.*
> *Dissection is a virtue when*
> *It operates on other men.*

Each day brings yet more scares – the newspapers are full of Frankenstein stories, conveying global threats from genetically modified food, failures of rail safety, air crashes, hurricanes off the Eastern coast of the United States, residues of nuclear pollution from the Chernobyl disaster in Ukraine still affecting Welsh mountains, virus mutations and the increasing inefficacy of antibiotics. . . . And then the stories about us – we're obese, eat too much salt or too little, take hardly any exercise, have become lousy parents. We can frighten ourselves into stupidity, too fearful to face daily life.

Many news stories contain grains of truth and we do need more awareness about global warming and the depletion of the ozone layer. We need to take necessary measures against harmful effects on the planet, but the overall Frankenstein effect doesn't help. It wears us down. Daily tragedies push us inexorably towards collective paralysis. The world is not at all how we imagined it to be, and never was or will be, but this seems to come as more of a shock to our generations. It had seemed that it was our planet, our world. It isn't ours. We have always 'belonged' to it rather than the other way around.

'God forbid that we should give out a dream of our own imagination for a pattern of the world' (Frances Bacon). The medieval essayist's comment is wasted on us. We want and even need the real world to reflect the patterns of our dreams. But dreams can turn into nightmares. Learning becomes largely a method of simply manipulating concepts, not about stripping away useless ideas. We get farther and farther away from ordinary living. Da Vinci saw that the best place to study spiders was in the hedgerow not a library. Nowadays there are probably more spiders in libraries than in the polluted hedgerows, but we know what he meant.

Kornfield (1993, p. 162) comments: 'The world is not supposed to be perfect according to our ideas. We have tried so long to change the world, yet liberation is not to be found by changing it, by perfecting it or ourselves. Whether we seek enlightenment through altered states or in community or in our everyday life, it will never come to us when we seek perfection.' The popularity of seeking perfection reflects a deep rejection of ordinary life and an inability to live in the present moment. We aren't dancing joyfully along the sandy beaches but poking and prodding nervously at life. It might bite us back. It is a symptom of our increasing anxiety and no sort of 'cure'. We are encouraged by the relevant professionals to examine our deficiencies, not to look at our strengths and resources. More crucially we reduce the diversity that contains the marvellous paradox of commonalties and differences and the real essence of humanity, one of many animals on this small blue planet.

The last words in Darwin's *On the Origin of Species*:

> *Thus, from the war of nature, from famine and death, the most exalted object which we are capable of conceiving, namely, the production of the higher animals, directly follows. There is a grandeur in this view of life, with its several powers, having been originally breathed into a few forms or into one; and that, whilst this planet has gone cycling on according to the fixed law of gravity, from so simple a beginning endless forms most beautiful and most wonderful have been, and are being, evolved.* (Darwin, 1964, p. 490)

We can be captured and enraptured by that simple and genuine magic.

Diversity is of profound importance. Gould comments on the reasons for saving species:

> *We relish diversity; we love every slightly different way, every nuance of form and behaviour – and we know that the loss of a significant fraction of this gorgeous variety will quench our senses and our satisfactions in any future meaningfully defined in human terms. What in the world could possibly be more magnificent than the fact that beetle anatomy presents itself in more than a half a million packages called species?*
> (Gould, 1994, p. 241)

We talk and write a great deal about improvement and progress. What are the measures? Do our methods of improvement work? Do they diminish essential diversity? Have we hit the designated targets and completed all the relevant tasks? Have these ways of calculated living, aiming to accomplish defined life tasks, proved 'successful'? For example our systems for improving mental health seem to be boomerang shaped.

> *Ironically, mental health education, which aims to teach people how to cope more effectively with life, has instead increased the demand for psychotherapeutic help. By calling attention to symptoms they might otherwise ignore and by labelling those symptoms as signs of neurosis, mental health education can create unwarranted anxieties, leading those to seek psychotherapy who do not need it. The demand for psychotherapy keeps pace with the supply, and at times one has the uneasy feeling that the supply may be creating the demand.* (Frank, quoted in Dineen, p. 195).

I have a strong sense that we are gradually diminishing ourselves.

Successful Picnics?

Can you measure all this? A Slovene friend told of a visit from an American academic. They went with his two young children for a picnic near Lake Bled. On the mountainside, in sight of the lovely lake, they ate sandwiches, drank orange juice, talked a lot and the children chased each other, and finally the sun set. On the way back to Ljubljana the American asked: 'Do you think that was a successful picnic?' What was the measure of success? Was it the number of sandwiches eaten; the amount of orange juice drunk; the noise of the children playing; the quality of academic discourse? Or does something essential evaporate the instant we ask these sorts of questions?

What does it mean to survive joyfully today? I don't really know and can offer no real'solutions', but I can ask what I hope are interesting questions. I'm no expert in living and certainly not any sort of guru, just someone struggling and occasionally surfing with life. My natural and inherent agnosticism makes me deeply suspicious of so-called 'solutions'. I deeply appreciate the many gifts of life – music, poetry, wind on the heath, the sound of the sea – all echoes of the Tao.

I've wrestled over many years with feelings of fear, anxiety and especially anger and rage. I'm a difficult person, a hedgehog living among moles, telling people things they don't want to hear. As a child I knew poverty and hardship. I was homeless, running away from my family to escape the surging violence and, as a reward, being beaten again by my father, dragged through despair and confusion, suicidal feelings, joy and ecstasy. My life is much of a mess rather like that of most people. 'The mass of men lead lives of quiet desperation' (Thoreau, 1960).

These sorrows and disappointments are the stuff of living. They are our human heritage. We are falling in love, falling out of love, getting sick, recovering, feeling lonely, despairing, feeling unappreciated. Quite recently, the feeling has developed that we can sometimes escape these sorrows, that life should mostly be lived contentedly, that we have almost a duty to be content and effective; that we can and even should exorcise the darker sides of our life with or without magic pills; that this darkness can be passed through and beyond lies harp music and honey sandwiches. Somehow life can and should be fixed.

Fixing life?

I'm even more suspicious of the syndromes than of the remedies. 'It's too easy to dismiss somebody else's lived experience as a symptom of this, that, or the other pathology: to label it, disinfect it, store it away neatly in slim buff files and prevent it making dangerous contact with the experience of normal people.' (Barker, 1998, p. 270). Barker rightly pathologises the whole process of diagnosis rather than people. Like him, I don't believe there is that much wrong with the way we live or are; not nearly as much as the soul hucksters would have us believe.

Rose comments more strongly:

These therapies of normality transpose the difficulties in living on to a psychological register; they become not intractable features of desire and frustration but malfunctions of the psychological apparatus that are remediable through the operation of particular techniques. The self is thus opened up, a new continent for exploitation by the entrepreneurs of the psyche, who both offer us an image of a life of maximized intellectual, commercial, sexual or personal fulfilment and assure us that we can achieve it with the assistance of the technicians of subjectivity. (Miller and Rose, 1986, p. 81–2).

We've got this desperate need to make headway. 'I've grown up you know. I've passed through a lot. I've made real progress. That was a difficult phase I was going through which is now ended.' It sounds like a therapeutic train running in Euro Disney. I am extremely dubious about ideas of personal progress and growth. Progress has become the ultimate contemporary illusion. In a century that has seen concentration camps and holocausts, we need to talk of human progress. It usually means banishing our darker selves to the nether regions; a way of disposing of unacceptable feelings.

Gould finds great dangers in progress.

Progress as a predictable result of ordered causes therefore becomes a double delusion – first because we must seek its cause more in the quirkiness of the wheel, turning tires into sandals and big brains towards fear of death, than in the plodding predictability of the wedge, propelling monkeys into men; secondly, because the supposed sweep of life towards progress only records our myopic focus on the right tail of a distribution whose mode has never moved from a prokaryotic cell. (Gould, 1994, p. 323)

These delusions involve the identification of a spine so that other events become peripheral.

Underlying dominant Western ideas are attempts to dispose of pain and suffering. We seek comfort and contentment, or in Watts's words:

to have pleasure without pain, wealth without poverty, and health without sickness. But as is now becoming obvious, our violent efforts to achieve this ideal with such weapons as DDT, penicillin, nuclear energy, automotive transportation, computers, industrial farming, damming, and compelling everyone by law, to be superficially 'good and healthy' are creating more problems than they solve. (Watts, 1979, p. 20)

Human beings cannot be 'fixed' by trained mechanics like broken cars in a garage. The dominant ideologies insist that almost everybody is broken. They involve an unceasing search for fresh syndromes and new methods of intervention. 'In principle, there is an assumption that all human problems can be converted into technical problems, and if the techniques to solve certain problems do not yet exist, then they will have to be invented. The world becomes ever more "makeable".' (Berger, 1977, p. 36). As Rose suggested earlier, everybody and everything is converted in to commodities for the purposes of buying and selling. We are surrounded by increasing numbers of psychological plumbers, electricians and mechanics loudly selling their wares and taking attention from the destructive structures that we could and should change.

I believe in the inalienable right to human unhappiness, like my favourite TV heroine 'Ally McBeal'. 'I know I'm in a mess but it's mine.' I've worked long years in nursing, social work and social care and was a therapist for over ten years. Most people I worked with professionally were poor and felt devalued. They were isolated and despairing. They suffered greatly from the greed of others. I've been a mental health survivor for more than 30 years and in broad opposition to ideologies that individualise social and economic problems. As the old song goes 'It's the poor that gets the blame'. The poor and distressed are not always with us. Hundreds of millions of people are unnecessarily distressed and sick, and many die needlessly. We watch hungry children in Africa on TV programmes and feel sorry and then disconnected. A BBC correspondent commented recently that African children look different, so it is very hard to identify with them. 'They don't look like us' meaning that they are black.

The Tao isn't simply passive and collusive. The 'Tao Te Ching' is surprisingly robust:

> *Why are people hungry?*
> *Because the rich take too much from them.*
> *This is why they don't have enough.*
> *Why are people rebellious?*
> *Because the powerful push them around.*
> *This is why they're angry.*

(Freke, 1995, p. 120)

Here we are being taught of empowerment. People don't have a fair share of the resources because relatively powerful people take more than their fair share. Poor people are rebellious because those who are rich and powerful push them around. It is very simple. This tradition of the wealthy causing poverty and then moralising at their expense is extremely long. The fourteenth-century poet William Langland (1959) wrote:

> *But beggars about midsummer go breadless to supper,*
> *And winter is worse, for they are wet-shod wanderers*
> *Frozen and famished and foully challenged*
> *And berated by richmen so that it is rueful to listen.*

Running away from a violent home and living on the streets and in hostels, I was acutely aware of the very mixed agendas of the Salvation Army and the Church Army. Nearly 700 years on, Langland would see much that was familiar. He would see *moralisers* writing newspaper editorials. He could talk with both evangelists and rescuers. *Evangelists* dressed in various garbs – primarily political or religious, using people living on the streets as a way of confirming their ideologies. *Rescuers* dump their own anger and frustration and greed of giving onto homeless people. Rescuers need victims. Both groups are tempted to stress their own wisdom and maturity and see homeless people largely in pathological ways.

Uncovering pathology and the associated labelling and blaming of 'patients' is extremely profitable. There are massive bucks to be made from persuading people that they are the victims of complex syndromes, invented only yesterday. Many people are delighted to be labelled, an aspect of sado–masochism, to be placed in a solid box. 'You're only the third case of Von Hauser's Syndrome we've diagnosed and the other two didn't have this same aggressive overlay and subtle complexity.' The poet T. S. Eliot describes the whole distressing process:

> *Half the harm that is done in this world*
> *Is due to people who want to feel important*
> *They don't mean to do harm –*
> *but the harm does not interest them,*
> *Or they do not see it, or they justify it*
> *Because they are absorbed in the endless struggle*
> *To think well of themselves.*

(Eliot, 1950, p. 111)

Healing and therapy have become very important vehicles for ambition, ways of achieving personal importance, any injury is either denied or not perceived. A dissident psychotherapist is even more cynical: 'In general, the power drive is given freest rein when it can appear under the cloak of objective and moral rectitude. People are the most cruel when they can use cruelty to enforce the "good".' (Guggenbühl-Craig, 1971, p. 10)

So-called compassion can cover many sins. Picardie, who was dying of cancer, had trouble with 'rubber neckers'.

> *X left a message last week and I had no idea who she was. I'm afraid I*
> *have no intention of going to the science museum with her, rude as that*
> *sounds. I am sick of being everybody's favourite cripple – you wouldn't*
> *believe the number of acquaintances who suddenly want to be your*
> *best friend and feel they're entitled to regular, blow by blow accounts*
> *of your emotional/physiological state. 'But Ruth, how ARE you?' they*
> *ask, meaningfully. 'Rubber neckers'.* (Picardie, 1998, p. 17–18)

They are voyeurs, living their lives through other people, the more distressed the better.

Cambridge scientists discover new syndrome
Most of this discovery of new syndromes and conditions has no scientific validity. We have little hard evidence of these supposed syndromes and even less to indicate that current techniques might be effective. Evidence-based clinical practise is in the very early stages of development. Many popular interventions are done with crossed fingers. People work in a massive industry with obscure products. Psychology, counselling, psychotherapy are all part of a billion-dollar-plus industry, employing hundreds of thousands of professionals, the great majority with a vested interest in uncovering vast tracks of pathology to help pay their mortgages. Sometimes in Cambridge, where I live, it feels that one half of the population is counselling the other half. They are searching for yet more customers after completing their diverse diplomas, certificates and degrees. They need a regular cash crop to pay for the frothy capuccinos.

These 'healing' professionals make a very comfortable living from this intense atmosphere of anxiety and uncertainty, of which the search for healing is one aspect. People seek any refuge from the rapidly changing times. We are persuaded that we live in an enormously dynamic period. We're all dizzy. Recently I visited a training centre for people with learning disabilities, to be told that things had been changing enormously. It's 30 years since I worked in such a centre but nothing much seems to have changed. I could have taken up the same job at 9 am next Monday morning without much trouble.

We believe that we're in a great flux – the World Wide Web, globalisation, mobile phones, the information revolution, robots. . . . I'm not sure it matters much, even if it proves to be true. My great great . . . grandfather, serving in

Cromwell's New Model army in the Civil War, probably felt similar storms; my Dad, serving in the Royal Air Force, went through a gigantic experience in World War II. It gives some sense of transient importance to be living in 'significant times'. What does it really mean except to express some anxiety about the future and satisfy the desire to be special?

The eighteenth-century poet Pope wrote: 'The proper study of Mankind is Man'. I can hear him laughing loudly and cynically right now. We've become totally obsessional. We want desperately to understand who and what we are, to have a way of living, but mostly to get rid of all the pain and anxiety. 'Lifestyle' is one word that sums it all up. We want to be fashionable and different. We want to be in charge, to possess many more bunches of bananas – the old-fashioned term is greed.

We try to control, conquer and overwhelm this small planet and ultimately the infinite galaxies beyond. We don't even have much control over ourselves. We get lost in our own shadows and are fearful of the dark. We're like a tiny white mouse on the huge head of a woolly mammoth. We scream out 'Left. Left. Right. Right. Straight on.' Every so often, by complete coincidence, the mammoth goes to the left or right whilst we are screaming 'Left' or 'Right.' So we think the beast is under control at last. We've finally cracked it. But at the next 'Straight on', it goes boldly rightwards.

In this greed for control, we easily fall prey to the powers of darkness. Conrad's dying Mr Kurtz was locked deep in the festering African jungle, with an insatiable greed for ivory. 'You should have heard him say, "My ivory." Oh yes, I heard him. "My intended, my ivory, my station, my river, my – " everything belonged to him – but that was a trifle. The thing was to know what he belonged to, how many powers of darkness claimed him for their own' (Conrad, 1973, p. 85). Now there's a good question – to what or whom do we belong? Kurtz was firmly in the grip of the ivory.

Tao
Central to this particular book is the term Tao. I won't try to define it because I'm not that stupid. I'd rather dance around it with various stories.

Chao-Chou asked, 'What is the Tao?'
The master [Nan-ch'uan] replied, 'Your ordinary consciousness is
the Tao.'
'How can one return into accord with it?'
'By intending to accord you immediately deviate.'

'But without intention, how can one know the Tao?'
'The Tao,' said the master, 'belongs neither to knowing nor to not
knowing. Knowing is false understanding; not knowing is blind
ignorance. If you really understand the Tao beyond doubt, it's like the
empty sky. Why drag in right and wrong?' (Watts, 1979, p. 38)

You see how Chao-Chou tries to pigeon hole it and Nan-ch'uan dances right
out of reach. Chou wants to get his philosophical scalpel and cut it into ten
thousand bits to discover how it all works. My younger brother Eric, when he
was six, did the same with alarm clocks but they didn't work on reassembly,
with dozens of small bits left over. Chou has this butterfly net, waves it
around in the direction of his teacher and completely misses, catching
himself. The Tao is not hard to define, just completely impossible. It's like a
fish trying to grasp the idea of water. Our linear way of thinking find circular
systems indescribable. Tao is too circular for conventional tape measures.

The farmer's horse ran away. That evening the neighbours gathered to
commiserate because it was such bad luck. He said 'May be.' The next
day the horse returned, but brought with it six wild horses, and the
neighbours exclaimed at his good fortune. And then, the following day,
his son tried to saddle and ride one of the wild horses, was thrown,
and broke his leg. Again the neighbours came to offer their sympathy
for his misfortune. He said, 'May be'. The day after, conscription
officers came to the village to seize young men for the army, but
because of his broken leg the farmer's son was rejected. When the
neighbours came in to say how fortunately everything had turned out,
he said, 'May be.' (Lin Yutang, 1938, p. 160).

This conveys the nature of never-ending events; nothing is ever really
finished. We slice thin pieces off to file in to various boxes. Every so-called
single event is part of something else. It points two fingers at the Tao.

Coming themes
So the rest of this book deals in more detail with these themes. The next
chapter is called 'mind dancing'. Ours is a serious but not earnest journey. We
need a sense of humour to make sense and nonsense of ourselves. Life makes
fun of us and we should help it. Humour turns us over like a pancake tossed in
the frying pan. We thought we knew this and that and suddenly life does a
back flip. It's not something on the very edge, to be indulged at certain times
and places, but something central to living. It isn't like luxury Swiss chocolate
eaten only at Christmas, but like bread and butter eaten every single day.

The story of Matzu, the great Zen teacher, pokes its rude finger through considerable fantasies. He strikes through cosmetic pretences with a sudden blow. He spies a poor holy sucker meditating on a rock. 'What are you doing?' he asks the poor schmuck, who replies 'I'm meditating.' 'Why?' probes Matzu. 'To become a Buddha,' says the human-tethered goat to the hungry tiger.

So Matzu starts slowly polishing a tile. 'What are you doing?' says his victim. 'I'm polishing this tile.' 'Why?' Says Matzu, 'To make a mirror out of it.' Says the schmuck, 'That's ridiculous. You'll never make a mirror out of a tile.' Delivering the punchy checkmate, Matzu comments: 'And all the meditating in the world will never make a Buddha out of you.'

Matzu sees through it all. He sees the gross attachment to meditation or psychotherapy, the obsession with some fixed point; the belief that the Tao is tarmacked, with double yellow stripes down the middle. Now we have become meditation junkies, still clutching onto ideas about the purpose and what might be achieved. *Mea culpa.* Our ideas about meditation and personal growth obscure the ordinary realities of everyday life. 'Throw it all away' Matzu shouts, more in hope than in reasonable expectation. I believe the fool continued meditating as if nothing had happened. He wanted to hang onto something, however useless. He mistook the pointing finger for the glowing moon.

Sometimes comedy is entirely serious. I have a soft spot for academic con-men. An American physicist, Sokal, was furious about the lack of rigour and hollowness of postmodernist philosophy. He wrote a hoax paper entitled 'Transgressing the Boundaries: Towards a Transformative Hermeneutics of Quantum Gravity' and sent it to *Social Text*, supposedly a learned postmodern journal. With considerable pride he afterwards described this paper as 'a melange of truths, half-truths, quarter-truths, falsehoods, non sequiturs, and syntactically correct sentences that have no meaning whatsoever'. Of course it was accepted and published some months later. Sokal wrote a splendid book called *Intellectual Impostures*. (Sokal and Bricmont, 1999). What a marvellous stunt to break through a dense forest of academic pomposity.

Chapter 3 describes 'temptations of perfection'. Our popular journals and magazines contain millions of powerful images of human beings. The women are mostly tall and slim, and always beautiful in an unanimated way. They are framed gorgeously against golden beaches or fashion hot spots. The men and women all seem to come from the TV show *BayWatch*. The men are tanned and heavily muscled with sixpack stomachs. There are mental equivalents of these paragons. They cope with life easily; they are always calm and serene, even in the midst of life's storms. These men and women are supermen and superwomen. They are not only lovely and handsome but seemingly talented as well. Glossy packaging is everything.

The authors of pop psychology books are mostly of the same breed. They write from high up in the clouds, mist hidden. They get there by spiritual helicopter rather than by scrambling up. Our knees are bloodied; theirs are pristine. They wear crisp white linen suits, a red rose in the buttonhole and have expensively coiffured hair – a million miles away from noisy city traffic jams, canned food with additives, screaming kids, TV game shows, packet soup and pot noodles. Their heads are eternally clear and fresh, full of the harmonies of Mozart's clarinet concertos. Even their voices have a superior, mystical ring from high spiritual and psychological plains to where we lie on our bellies in the mud on the valley bottom.

They are very special people, never squandering valuable time. They use time management, wave electronic organisers and jog vigorously to work just in time for a healthy muesli breakfast. (I jog regularly) Their mountain-top instructions are clearly heard because they have taken elocution lessons, and when young wore braces on their teeth. They invoke us to become smarter; to get up much earlier in the morning – the early worm catches the bird; take freezing cold showers three times daily; concentrate more fully; do exercises; breathe much more deeply. . . . These peak-top travellers are regular smart arses.

These gods and goddesses have mature and lasting relationships and make excellent parents. Everyone loves and admires them. Of course they don't exist in any real world. Every so often a magazine exposes them mercilessly as less than ordinary human beings, with drink and drug problems and a tendency to lose their rag, eat live hamsters and frequently have unsafe sex with the wrong people.

This pursuit of perfection, increasingly common in both physical and psychological ways, is very dangerous. We spend our money on plastic surgery, struggling vainly against gravity, and now even have the prospect of changing our genes. We try to improve our mental state through a myriad of expensive and doubtful methods. It is a clear route for non-acceptance of who and what we are.

I much prefer the Zen earthquake story. The master was showing some young people around the old monastery. During their visit there was an earthquake. After it was over he got them together. 'Now you've seen that we deal with an earthquake mindfully. I took you immediately into the kitchen because it's the safest place and we got down on the floor. The only sign of agitation was that I drank a glass of water.' 'Excuse me,' said one young visitor, 'that wasn't water. It was a whole glass of soy sauce.' So much for mindful practice!

'Vulnerability as strength' is the next theme (Chapter 4). This borrows strongly from shamanic traditions. It provides an antidote to healing through increased strength and wisdom, the powerful message in the West. Much genuine healing comes from unknowing and from being vulnerable. Many human problems come from forms of disconnectedness and imbalance. The 'Tao Te Ching' sees great danger in striving for better and better states.

> *Give up trying to seem holy,*
> *forget trying to appear wise,*
> *and it will be a lot better for everyone.*
> *Abandon trying to seem good,*
> *throw out self-righteousness,*
> *and rediscover natural compassion.*
> *Stop trying to be so smart,*
> *quit being calculating,*
> *and you won't become a rogue.*

(Freke, 1995, p. 54)

This makes a vital distinction between wisdom and cleverness. It raises the issue of striving and/or intentionality. The more we struggle to be better or wiser, the more we are bound to fail. Another early Taoist text is almost as dismissive in explaining vitality or prime energy.

> *When there is thought, there is knowledge,*
> *But when there is knowledge, then you must stop.*
> *Whenever the forms of the mind have excessive knowledge,*
> *You lose your vitality.*

(Roth, 1999, p. 60)

The message is a difficult one for Western minds. Allow natural spontaneity to arise rather than this constant and exhausting effort to be better than we essentially are, warping our original nature. Give up trying to be saintly. Very few of us, if any, are genuine saints. This so-called Higher Way can easily lead to self-righteousness; to a feeling of smugness. Enjoy your own authentic stupidity rather than strive vainly to be wise.

The 'Yin of Flowing' (Chapter 5) gets close to the essential Tao; not doing or imposing, but flowing. All our spanners and screwdrivers will do us no good. Life is a current in which we all swim and eventually drown. We can struggle in it, try to impose our will, but the river flows heavily and smoothly, quickly and slowly. It would be wiser to feel and enjoy its nature rather than try to control or understand it. A good swimmer moves in harmony with the water. This involves moving in tune with its currents.

We can't all do it our way, however beautifully old Sinatra crooned. The Tao has its way. We are not only a part of the Tao; we are the Tao and in no way separate from it and that is the first essential barrier to study. We cannot stand aside and hope to hear the music; to listen to the great river of life, to the flowing of the water. It has its own directions and inherent nature. It is about needs, not wanting or having. We can give up the desire to control, or rather let it just melt away.

'Yang of discipline' (Chapter 6) completes the Yin/Yang dyad. Flowing isn't about letting everything hang out, making love not war. Discipline is currently having a bad press. Individuality means we do what we fancy. Not at all. The Tao requires very considerable internal discipline, mainly in the giving up of our ideas. Meditation practice doesn't involve some grandiose notion of some higher state (whatever that might mean) but a practice changing our whole relationship to Nature and to other sentient beings.It happens in the present moment. There is no other time but the present. We learn to live in this moment, none other. Part of that means giving up precious ideologies – the internal acquisitions, much more sticky than material objects such as cars and boats.

The third Zen patriarch said: 'Do not search for the truth; Only cease to cherish opinions.' (Sengstan, in Brandon, 1985b, p. 9).

Paying attention – mindfulness – is the key to the spiritual way of life. We need, but stoutly resist the constant practise of mindfulness in everyday activities such as cooking and cleaning, which spreads out from formal meditation and pays attention, brings full energy to our daily living, especially to what and who is right in front of us. Our minds become still so we can really hear and experience what Nature is sending. In that stillness we experience the subtleties of change, the universe actually breathing; understand that it is part of us and we are immersed in it. Nothing is separate.

To be filled with the masculine power of Yang,
follow the feminine nature of Yin,
Be empty like a valley,
Where water gathers to form a stream,
Gather Natural Goodness,
Until you are like a little child again.

(Freke 1995 pge 65)

The spiritual road is about living out our *uniqueness,* not our individualism. We are all of us different and need to celebrate that overall and wonderful diversity. But we do need commonality as well as difference. The elements that connect can be healing and wholesome. We struggle hard to be different, to be increasingly unique. We industriously pursue the goal of the extraordinary like a car mechanic. But we are not custom-built cars. We are already unique before the moment of birth, extraordinary and also very similar. The modern disease is 'individuality'. We are struggling to be different and distinctive, part of this enormous global diversity, which our struggle reduces. Recall the old Chinese saying: 'We are all islands in the one great sea.' We can just be – rather than become anybody or anything. Paradoxically the more we strive to be different, the more we are the same. Look at all those teenagers all over the world, trying to be different individuals but wearing very similar jeans or chinos and T shirts.

The spiritual way is *nothing special* at all. We make a great song and dance about it as 'the road less travelled', but it contains no showy magic, cheap or expensive gimmicks, or even motorway restaurants. It has no religious fireworks, spiritual miracles or anything of much interest. It's just ordinary, walking the road, playing with the dog, paying attention, often boring, living in the present moment. Nothing to write home to Mum about. Blink twice and you'd miss it.

Its elements are so mundane, so ordinary – it's easy to miss them. It's easy to miss the ordinary everyday miracles whilst looking for a rare eclipse. Zen Master Rinzai said:

> *Just be your ordinary selves in an ordinary life, wear your robes and*
> *eat your food, and having nothing further to seek, peacefully pass your*
> *time. From everywhere you have come here; all of you eagerly seek the*
> *Buddha, the Dharma, and deliverance; you seek to escape from the*
> *Three Worlds. You foolish people, if you want to get out of the Three*
> *Worlds, where then can you go?'* (Schloegl, 1975, p. 22)

There is no escape from this everyday life. Nobody understands or doesn't understand anything. Don't be concerned or unconcerned with what is special or even attempt to understand. Just clean the room, wash your clothes, wash up, cook a meal, eat and then go and serve all sentient beings.

> *Ch'ing, the chief carpenter, was carving wood from a stand for hanging musical instruments. When finished, the work appeared to those who saw it as though of supernatural execution. And the prince of Lu asked him, saying, 'What mystery is there in your art?' 'No mystery, your Highness,' replied Ch'ing; 'and yet there is something. When I am about to make such a stand, I guard against any diminution of my vital power. I first reduce my mind to absolute quiescence. Three days in this condition, and I become oblivious of any reward to be gained. Five days, and I become oblivious of any fame to be acquired. Seven days, and I become unconscious of my four limbs and my physical frame. Then, with no thought of the Court present in my mind, my skill becomes concentrated, and all disturbing elements from without are gone. I enter some mountain forest. I search for a suitable tree. It contains the form required, which is afterwards elaborated. I see the stand in my mind's eye, and then set to work. Otherwise, there is nothing. I bring my own natural capacity into relation with that of the wood. What was suspected to be of supernatural execution in my work was due solely to this.'* (Chuang-tzu, quoted in Giles, 1972, p. 240–1).

So now you know everything. What exactly do you know? Does it involve looking at the finger or the moon? Does it really matter? If it's glowing reasonably brightly, that's probably the moon. Very few fingers are made of green cheese, so you could tell with a single bite. After seven very long days of sitting on your bum, you'll be so numb you wouldn't care at all.

Chapter 2
Mind Dancing

All beauty, all music, all religion; all poetry, is a dancing of the mind.
Without this dancing of the spirit there is no true Zen

(Blyth, 1960, p. 35).

Counselling and psychotherapy have a dusty and worthy image. They are portrayed as solemn and grim occupations by their practitioners – heavy steamed dumplings rather than palate-melting soufflès. Psychologists and social workers have never been highly rated for their sense of the ludicrous. You have to feel reasonably secure to make fun of yourself. Security is in short supply in these professions, but in carefully avoiding banana skins you risk getting a custard pie in the face. 'Humour is the only test of gravity, and gravity the only test of humour. For a subject which will not bear raillery is suspicious; and a jest which will not bear a serious examination is certainly false wit' (Leontinus, quoted in Blyth, 1960, p. 56).

A brief time ago our practice contained some serious absurdities. The personal growth boom of the 1960s and early 1970s dragged some of us from badly lit consulting rooms into nude marathon encounter groups and a whole host of other diverting forms of therapy by the sunny sides of swimming pools. We were living in the damp town of Preston at the time. They were part orgy (though we never saw much of that) and part journey into inner space. Even those fleeting adventures were laced with old-fashioned, inverted puritanism. Any incidental enjoyment was drowned in a compulsion to be spontaneous and insightful. 'Come on. Be more spontaneous!' Nowadays, regretfully, we have sunk into a quagmire of self-importance, verging on pomposity.

I much prefer gallows humour, once so common in mental hospitals and other grim institutions. It had an intense vigour.

Jimmy McKenzie was a bloody pest at the mental hospital because he went around shouting back at his voices. We could only hear one end of the conversation, of course, but the other end could be inferred in general terms at least from:

'Away ye fuck, yet filthy minded bastards . . .'

It was decided at one and the same time to alleviate his distress and ours, by giving him the benefit of a leucotomy.

An improvement in his condition was noted.

19

After the operation he went around no longer shouting abuse at his voices, but: 'What's that? Say that again! Speak up ye buggers, I cannae hear ye!' (Laing, 1967, p. 146)

Jimmy was obviously ready for serious social work training! His communication wasn't going through a dozen professionalised filters, removing any discernible risks.

Over twenty years ago I talked with a young social work student at the Lancaster Moor mental hospital. She complained about the various hospital professionals, including me. 'You don't take the work seriously. You don't recognise their pain and suffering.' I asked her to explain. 'You're always laughing and making jokes.' I pointed out the distinction between earnest and serious but it was all a waste of time. Despite her accusations, we took the work very seriously but also knew we were living close to farce. She was involved in a sprint and ours was a marathon. The humour recognised the impossibilities of our work. Daily we faced profound human suffering and neglect in a place that was doing enormous damage to people – not just the patients but also the staff.

> *Illness tossed you over the rails*
> *of our world –*
> *the huge hospital swallowed you*
> *then swam away*
> *to go through its routines with you*
> *deep and distant.*
>
> (Ransford, in Downie, 1994, p. 154)

I'd like see the late Ruth Picardie go ten rounds with my earnest student.

'A few people, I think, reckon that cripples can help them get to heaven, including my born-again former school teacher who this week sent me a book of 'true life stories of Christians who have all experienced tragedy of one sort or another . . . all of them have found hope in their suffering through knowing God who suffered first.' In an accompanying letter, she urged me to allow the peace of God into my heart at this difficult time. To her, I say, sorry, Miss, but I was the one who carved '666' on the desks, I'm still half-Jewish (sadly the wrong half) and no death-bed conversion looms, despite the scary grim reaper ad.' (Picardie, 1998, p. 73).

One major discovery after nearly 40 years was that clients' ability to get into trouble always exceeds the facility of professionals to rescue them. Of course they're really supposed to rescue themselves, as in the story of the two

Rogerian therapists. These two wise men were standing by a large pond discussing the finer points of non-intervention. They observed in the distance a woman struggling in deep water. She seemed to be in trouble and there was a fierce struggle, her arms waving for a few moments until all was silent in the mixture of water and weed. After several moments of contemplation one therapist commented: 'What a shame she didn't cry out for help.'

Serious jokes

Trungpa writes directly about seeing through the great joke:

> *So a sense of humor is not merely a matter of trying to tell jokes or make puns, trying to be funny in a deliberate fashion. It involves seeing the basic irony of the juxtaposition of extremes, so that one is not caught taking them seriously, so that one does not take seriously their game of hope and fear. This is why the experience of the spiritual path is so significant, why the practice of meditation is the most insignificant experience of all. It is insignificant because you place no value judgement on it. Once you are absorbed into that insignificant situation of openness without involvement in value judgement, then you begin to see all the games going on around you. Someone is trying to be stern and spiritually solemn, trying to be a good person. Such a person might take it seriously if someone offended him, might want to fight. If you work in accordance with the basic insignificance of what is, then you begin to see the humor in this kind of solemnity, in people making such a big deal about things.'* (Trungpa, 1987, p. 115).

He points to the essential pomposity and absurdity of our professions. Every profession has a vibrant version of the policeman's imagined thin blue line. I never visited or worked with any organisation for the homeless that didn't believe it took in the people that 'nobody else would touch.' Most of us have to believe in our singular importance; that we stand as warriors, the last line of defence against overwhelming forces.

> *Then out spake brave Horatius,*
> *The Captain of the Gate;*
> *'To every man upon this earth*
> *Death cometh soon or late,*
> *And how can Man die better,*
> *Than by facing fearful odds,*
> *For the ashes of his fathers*
> *And the temples of his Gods.'*

(Macaulay, 1993 p. 148)

Some of us earn a reasonable living by charging distressed people folding money for simply talking to us. We mostly listen and they mostly talk about loneliness, despair, having little intimacy, not being understood by 'significant' others. Our heads nod gently and our mouths go 'hmmm' and 'hmmm'. One of my early counsellors nodded off during one session. I went babbling on regardless.

Several years later in the Manjushri Buddhist centre in the Lake District I was doing a long period of silence. I sat in their beautiful grounds with a card round my neck: 'David is doing a period of silence.' Several people I'd previously counselled came to talk. It was relaxing just to listen and not to have to think of something wise to say. One told me afterwards, in rather a back-handed compliment, that it was the best session she'd ever had.

We are all pioneers of a sort – rough frontiersmen and women. The so-called helping professions are at the beginning of an exciting journey, that attempts to explore and enlarge human awareness and establish new disciplines – echoing some of the experiences of sixteenth-century physics. It is a fresh form of alchemy. There is that same sense of arrant nonsense and profound wisdom jostling side by side – often very difficult to tell which is which.

Mostly the picture is of isolated and earnest therapists and social workers, silently inventing overcomplicated theories, facing distressed clients and both agonising eternally. It is rather more like chess than dance. Vicarious suffering meets individualised pain – the fixed grimace rather than the spontaneous smile. The mouth may smile but the eyes rarely. Professionals, all of whom presumably had a traumatic time in training, often with a sodding miserable Middle European teacher, seek unconsciously to wreak some vengeance in turn on their own students and subjects. And so the negative karma continues.

Psychotherapists are rarely writers, poets or musicians, with ability to capture the butterfly-wing quality of dynamic encounters with people. My experience of meeting with distressed people owes more to the Marx Brothers than to Karl Marx or Sigmund Freud. I suspect that therapy sessions with large helpings of frothy bubble and joy are considerably more typical than the po-faced and respectable accounts common in the books. Of course there is considerable suffering but many sessions are punctuated with jokes and laughter.

Some years ago I visited a bright young lady at her home. She was cancer-riddled, had about two weeks to live and was just about to enter a hospice.

Her mother, a devout Roman Catholic, was painfully angry. She was especially furious that her daughter had summonsed me – a Buddhist monk. I was adding to the already immense problems. The atmosphere was deeply fraught.

Lying quietly upstairs in her bedroom, the daughter asked weakly, 'I would really like to learn to meditate. Can you teach me?' I replied 'Aren't you cutting it a bit fine?' The acute tension was suddenly released. We both collapsed with laughter and took several minutes to recover. She was the best student I've ever had. Her concentration was completely undivided and she died peacefully a few days later.

Humour and laughter aren't chocolate and whipped cream in therapy but the genuine bread and butter, milk and apples. They aren't optional luxuries, only to be indulged in after several hours of bawling your eyes out. Laughter doesn't have to be painfully earned. It comes bubbling up like a warm spring. Humour is the core. It's yeast that gives life to important processes by which we expand our awareness of ten thousand different realities – all inconsistent with one another. Through humour, we toss life in the air lightly like a pancake and flip it neatly over, eventually becoming the pancake ourselves.

Butterflies and buffalo
Humour can help free us from many fixed illusions. It shakes our attachment to the ego. We don't know whether we are Chou or the butterfly, or even whether it matters.

> *Once I dreamt that I was a butterfly, fluttering here and there; in all ways a butterfly. I enjoyed my freedom as a butterfly, not knowing that I was Chou. Suddenly I awoke and was surprised to be myself again. Now can I tell whether I was a man who dreamt that he was a butterfly, or whether I am a butterfly who dreams that she is a man? Between Chuang Chou and the butterfly there must be differentiation. [Yet in the dream nondifferentiation takes place.] This is called interfusion of things.* (Chung-yuan, 1975, p. 20)

Now for a timely warning: the 'Tao Te Ching' of Lao-tzu (who almost certainly never existed), whose quotes adorn many of these pages, and Chuang Tzu are not to be taken too seriously for the sake of your spiritual health. You can hear these ancient Chinese guys laughing on almost every line. Watts (19798, p.79) puts it uncharacteristically soberly: 'It must be understood, in passing, that both Lao-tzu and Chuang Tzu enjoy the humor of overstating their case – the latter sometimes choosing truly preposterous examples to illustrate a point.' What's a butterfly between friends?

Humour provides an immensely earthy challenge to established realities and concepts. Somehow, in the same moment we can be both in the clouds and standing firmly on the earth. Life is never as we imagined or expected it to be. In one single moment we are surrounded by immensely high stone walls, topped by the electrified barbed wire of human suffering. There seems no possible escape, only dreary life imprisonment. In the same moment, the walls and wire fall down in a large pile of rubble, turning into a giant rubber duck, topped by a face that looks exactly like our own.

A highly anxious and painfully thin young man came to see me. He was accompanied by agitated parents, who talked incessantly. During this long interview, I too felt nervous. Their son was an elective mute, labelled 'acute schizophrenic' by a local psychiatric service. They carried a heavy sheaf of letters, mostly on headed notepaper, from various expensive and well-qualified professionals to whom he had steadfastly refused to say a single word. It must have been very annoying. He hadn't spoken to anyone for more than fifteen months. As a final act of desperation he was admitted compulsorily to a local mental hospital and subsequently refused to eat or speak, apparently in mute protest. One morning he'd walked the ten miles home in the pouring rain. His parents were in despair and asked whether I would see him regularly as a last hope. I said that was fine if it was fine with him, and he came alone.

He came alone the second time, much to my relief – a slow and ungainly figure. I had run the term 'elective mutism' through an expensive medical computer programme. It's best to let computers take the strain of anxiety. It presented a single miserly reference. Apparently the Sioux (Native Americans) when under stress because of the declining buffalo herds, went collectively and electively mute during the last century. Professionally, I was not yet clear about how to use this genuine nugget of information. It was obviously just a single confusing piece in a great jigsaw. In preparation I provided an impressive array of felt-tip pens of various colours and several large notepads, not especially to sketch herds of buffalo, which probably died out several thousand years ago in the north-west of England, but more pro-saically to write words such as Yes and No.

He waited silently, sitting sideways to me and avoiding my gaze. His eyes closely examined the ceiling in our classic Victorian room. I was surprisingly nervous once more and so took up the orthodox psychotherapist's stance – when feeling completely ignorant, look as dignified and distinguished as possible, which gets easier upon growing into grey-haired middle age. I learnt such tricks from watching my old Bede Grammar School headmaster, who was always slow and dull. It took me ages to work out that he was also stupid. I spoke solemnly, slowly and extremely clearly.

'I'm so glad you came. I want to compile a full record of your life. I need a long conversation with your mother because she probably knows you best. It will help our sessions together. Can I have your permission? Will you please write down Yes or No on these pages?' After a seeming age, whilst he sat wistfully and motionlessly, a low but firm voice from somewhere in the room said 'No.' I was startled. After all, there were only the two of us. 'What do you mean – No?' Again, he responded, after another long wait – very slowly and quietly, 'No. There's no need. I'll tell you all that you want to know.'

'Why haven't you talked to people before?' He replied slowly but very clearly: 'They didn't want to listen.' His slow and scratchy voice ran round and round my empty head. My immediate response was a considerable mixture of pride and anger. I looked a genuine fool with all the different coloured felt-tips and big notepads, like a timekeeper at the Olympics, much too late for the race. Now my detailed and intimate knowledge of the Sioux was rendered useless at a stroke.

And then flooded in overwhelming feelings of hubris. Great! I alone had cracked it. Cracked it – because of my unique personal qualities and profound skills. He'd spoken directly to me where all those eminent psychiatrists had failed. He'd recognised me as someone special. Yet another scalp was on the wall. I looked at him and we both saw how ridiculous the whole situation was and laughed for a long time. My professional posture, good only for short sprints, had self-destructed.

Psychotherapeutic ideologies discourage dancing barefoot in the long wet grass. How can you dance to the tune of my favourite social work term – 'ongoing dyadic relationships'? Would you feel 'ambivalent' about it? This language doesn't smell of new-mown hay, lavender, buttercups and spiders webs on wet hawthorn bushes. It contains little feeling for chamber music. It smells sourly of duty and obligation, with a stale odour of original teutonic terms – the angst of these human professions. Basic words such as analysis, therapy, counselling, catharsis, transference and so on have a righteous feel. They are the purgative elixirs of human growth. The taste is so dreadful it must be doing some good.

In the West, at least in fuzzy New Age circles, spirituality is eminently fashionable. It is perceived as precious and highly desirable, like a fine chocolate powder sprinkled over a stodgy pudding to give a special flavour. Take this passage from a popular counselling text:

> *It is clear to me now that the decision to trust the feeling of interrelated-ness was the first step towards a willingness on my part to acknowledge my spiritual experience of reality and to capitalise on the many hours spent in prayer and worship. It was as if previously I had refused to draw on this whole area of awareness in the conduct of my therapeutic work. In my zeal not to proselytise it was as if I had deliberately deprived myself of some of the most precious resources in the task of relating to my clients. Once I had opened myself to myself, however, I was capable of experiencing the communion of souls, or the member-ship of one of another, which is the fundamental given of the spiritual life.* (Mearns and Thorne, 1988, p. 37)

Note the language used in this classy nonsense – 'my spiritual experience' is to be 'capitalised' on. The language is that of the hypermarket. Phrases such as 'my clients', 'opened myself to myself' and 'to trust the feeling of inter-relatedness' sound unlike the music of spirituality but of inflating egos, the use of crude tools applied to the client. Nothing in genuine spirituality prepares the student for hammers and spanners.

Many writers claim a revival of interest. 'Many people are searching for spiritual meaning and an ontological significance in their lives. . . . The religious movement is beginning to make its appearance felt in professional social work thinking and education for practice' (Siporin, 1985). It is unclear whether this is a fervent wish or a practical reality. I see no great surge of genuine interest, but a simple changing of fashions.

Hear the loud and authentic cackle in this Chuang Tzu story:

> *There was a man who was so disturbed by the sight of his shadow and so displeased with his own footsteps that he determined to get rid of both. The method he hit upon was to run away from them. So he got up and ran. But every time he put his foot down there was another step, while his shadow kept up with him without the slightest difficulty.*

> *He attributed his failure to the fact that he was not running fast enough. So he ran faster and faster, without stopping, until he finally dropped dead. He failed to realize that if he merely stepped into the shade, his shadow would vanish, and if he sat down and stayed still, there would be no more footsteps.* (Merton, 1965, p. 155)

26

There is a Sufi story in a similar vein involving that wise fool – the Mulla Nasrudin. His students discovered him on hands and knees in the courtyard of his house. 'What are you doing?' 'I'm looking for my lost key.' Enthusiastically they all join his search for the lost key. After a long while, someone asks sensibly 'Where exactly did you lose it?' The mulla says 'Over there' pointing to the other side of the courtyard. 'Then why are we all searching over here.' Says the mulla, 'Because there is more light over here.' These students didn't understand anything. They thought the task was to find a lost key and open the door. For the mulla this was a test, about working together and remaining in the light.

Are we running away from our shadows because we can't think of anything else? Or is it just fear? Surely we realise this strategy can't succeed. Are we simply searching over in the light because we're told to do so and it's where everyone else is looking? 'I know it's over there because that's where everyone is.' We are afraid to stick out in the crowd, to take up unpopular causes. So we are condemned eternally to search uselessly among the crowds, rather than where the key was lost, in the certain knowledge we'll never find it.

We know the answer to the riddle the mulla set many centuries ago. Growth can take place everywhere and anywhere depending on our attitude and skills, and yet we still associate growth with pain. Somehow we've learned to trust tears and fears and mistrust both laughter and joy. If someone is crying in deep sorrow, they are obviously facing up to some harsh realities, because they are having a bad time.

Harsh realities
Must 'realities' be so harsh? If we are relaxing, laughing, enjoying ourselves, we are obviously escaping from something deep and painful. But why? If laughter can be an escape from difficult and unpleasant realities, then so can crying and pain. Are misery and mania so different? I see more people running away in tears than running away in laughter. What prevents jokes and joy from being a floral gateway into new perceptions any less than tears and pain?

Take this story from hostages Brian Keenan and John McCarthy in Lebanon, the morning after being beaten up by their guards.

> *The next morning was full of surprises. Not least John's first remark to me as he raised his blindfold. 'Oh holy fuck, your body looks like blackberry and custard pudding . . . How's your feet?' he continued. I answered dryly, admiring his remark. 'Well, I'll not be skipping the light fantastic for a while! How are you?' I asked him. 'I'm fine,' he*

answered, 'I didn't get it as bad as you.' 'Bollocks, you're always trying to be better than everybody else, John.' Our humour was not heroism, quite the reverse. It was a way of putting the previous night at a distance from us, screened behind humour and affection, so we could take control of it before it took control of us. (Keenan, 1992, p. 245)

Were they using humour as a method of escape? They were certainly using it to bond together as well as to make some sense of what had happened.

When we lose sight of the far horizon, we can also lose our sense of humour, of proportion. We lose our ability to roll over and over, seeing the world and ourselves from many different and disturbing angles. We can no longer see the cosmic joke. The joyous mystery has fled and only oceans of self-pity remain. The sparkle and lightness have disappeared. We take ourselves all too earnestly, much of the time.

> *I remember, I remember,*
> *The fir trees dark and high;*
> *I used to think their slender tops*
> *Were close against the sky;*
> *It was a childish ignorance,*
> *But now 'tis little joy*
> *To know I'm farther off from heav'n*
> *Than when I was a boy.*
>
> (Thomas Hood, 1993 p. 145)

In my own years of severe depression every morning seemed grey, even when the sun shone brightly. I found it difficult to appreciate anything or anybody – the flowers in the garden, the taste of an orange, the love of a friend, the nourishment from my loving wife. For me, every slight movement was an effort. I drowned in misery. I couldn't make any sense of how or why other people found ordinary life so enjoyable. What did they find to enjoy? I was envious, puzzled and often furious. I couldn't begin to see the wonderful and changing world as they saw and felt it. Instead I was full of enormous rage about life – that I'd been let down. Life had failed to deliver what I'd expected. I had, without intention, built a grim prison.

Without that ordinary humour our mind loses the capacity to move in a thousand different directions, to laugh at its own weaknesses and stupidities. We call that process negative and destructive self-talk – becoming de-pressed. We are pressed down in a hundred different ways. One major indication of that oppression lies in dragging ourselves heavily through life, hardly able to hold the mind together from one moment to the next. Getting through each day requires a supreme effort. Yesterday, last week or month or year, we walked the high tightrope of ordinary life without even realising the difficulties. We didn't give it a second thought. Now it's immensely complex, our minds splinter rapidly and we could fall to the ground at any moment.

Humour involves that gossamer subtlety of shifting through different realities without making a judgement of what is more or less real. Shakespeare said: 'There is nothing either good or bad but thinking makes it so.' The tufts of that flexibility of mind float lightly on the breeze. Weighed down with self-consciousness, heavy fears and ideas, we cannot fly at all. We are blinkered with only the most restricted views. Our minds become chronically conditioned. Suddenly, through a flash of humour, the world can turn on its axis and we see everything from a startling new and wider angle. What we'd thought was everything is now seen as only a tiny splinter of the expanding universe.

Chogyam Trungpa, a late great Tibetan lama, linked this suffocating process with 'Big Me' – 'having to be good, having to behave myself.' (Trungpa, 1987, p. 111–9). This sort of moral straitjacket is the Black Parrot. It sits on my shoulder screeching out my failings and shortfalls. At all costs I have to 'do it right', whatever that might mean. The spiritual pathway can easily become a souped up exercise in 'doing it right' to the power of ten million, not a genuine search for truth but hollow acting and posturing. Humour sees directly beyond that crude duality, observing both situational poles as they really are.

Take this story of a monk trying to impress his patron who provides everything material.

> There was a hermit whose devotee lived several miles away in a village. This devotee supported the hermit, supplying him with food and other necessities of life. Most of the time the devotee sent his wife or daughter or son to bring the hermit supplies; but one day the hermit heard that the donor himself was coming. He thought, 'I must impress him, I must clean and polish the shrine objects and make the shrine very neat and my room extremely tidy.'
>
> So he cleaned and re-arranged everything until his shrine looked very impressive with bowls of water and butter lamps burning brightly. And when finished he sat down and began to admire the room and look around. Everything looked very neat, somehow unreal, and the shrine appeared unreal as well. Suddenly, to his surprise, he realised that he

*was being a hypocrite. Then he went into the kitchen and got handfuls
of ashes and threw them all over the shrine until his room was a
complete mess.*

*When his patron came, he was extremely impressed by the natural
quality of the room, by it being so untidy. The hermit could not hold
himself together. He burst into laughter and said, 'I tried to tidy both
myself and my room, but then I thought perhaps I should show it to you
this way.' And so they both, patron and hermit, burst into laughter.*
(Trungpa, 1987, pp. 117–8)

All of us can identify with this. It's the great struggle with the 'Big Me'. We
have become firmly attached to particular images of ourselves, so we sell
people attractively packaged icons – reflecting how we wish to be seen,
cunningly concealing the inconsistencies and brutalities. There is a sophisticated social game in which the talker and the listener collude. 'I'm not like
that. I'm really like this . . . I'm not untidy, I'm really tidy and neat. I'm not
aggressive. . . .'

When we misbehave, slip outside of careful packaging, we learn to comment
internally: 'That wasn't really me. I don't know what came over me. . . .' We
go to painful and careful lengths to develop mirages, to deceive people rather
than simply be as we are, whatever sort of chaos that might mean. In playing
these social games over many years, we can lose intimacy with ourselves,
begin to believe our own press releases.

For the monk the situation was plainly ridiculous. He had spent a considerable
time tidying his room and small shrine to impress his patron. Then he saw it
was hypocrisy and that he was pretending to be somebody and something he
wasn't. So he decided just to let things hang loose. Throwing the ashes around
and making a bigger mess, taking his manipulative hypocrisy out of the dark
cupboard and risking showing it – the result had still impressed! What
impressed most was that he was comfortable with his immense stupidity. The
patron loved him because he was not as he might have been.

Oh for the joys of such mischief – of throwing over the social straitjackets
and dancing barefoot in the wet.

> *When I am an old woman I shall wear purple*
> *With a red hat which doesn't go, and doesn't suit me.*
> *And I shall spend my pension on brandy and summer gloves*
> *And satin sandals, and say we've got no money for butter.*

I shall sit down on the pavement when I'm tired
And gobble up samples in shops and press alarm bells
And run my stick along the railings
And make up for the sobriety of my youth.
I shall go out in my slippers in the rain
And pick flowers in other people's gardens
And learn to spit.

(Jenny Joseph, quoted in Downie, 1994, p. 35 – 6)

Joy and play

Thich Nhat Hanh, the Vietnamese Zen teacher, wrote: 'Life is filled with suffering, but it is also filled with many wonders, like the blue sky, the sunshine, the eyes of a baby. To suffer is not enough. We must also be in touch with the wonders of life. They are within and all around us, everywhere, any time.' (Hanh, 1982, p. 3). Pleasures and pain come equally to us. One day it rains; the next day the sun shines. We have to avoid getting hooked on rain or pain, sun or pleasure. Whatever comes can be equal to us, is important for our learning.

To become a part of the planet's wonders, both inside and outside, we need to learn to dance and play like small children. We need to recognise our fragility, to value our inconsistencies, to live daily with our mysteries. 'Ring-a-ring-a roses – all fall down.' We can learn to wheel and whirl, everything from the foxtrot to rock and roll to the cha cha, but particularly to relearn the dance from our birth. That means really hearing the natural music of our life and moving in harmony with it. Our bodies sway subtly like leaves in an autumn wind – spiritual Fred Astaires and Ginger Rogers – wheeling and whirling away into nothing at all.

So many of the people who came through our front door in Preston for psychotherapy sessions had never learned to play. They didn't know how to magic a vast and ever changing universe from a few wooden bricks and a tin of soap bubbles or to conjure up a rail network from a row of old shoe boxes. They didn't know how to move in subtle circles or hold hands in fairy rings, or receive a foot massage, or spend days talking to fantasy rabbits. They only knew how to be responsible, how to make money, how to sit on committees; most of all, how to be what others thought they ought to be. Perhaps they'd dreamed as small children of kite-flying over the Andes, but now they were qualified accountants, social workers or worse still estate agents, and supposed to behave themselves.

Real and creative playing is essential for spiritual growth; in fun, throwing ourselves into the flow of life; the fount of flexibility of thought and movement. We can forget ourselves completely in the absorption of the moment. We learn to move in a myriad ways and simply create. For many, even leisure has become just another way of achieving yet more, of destroying ourselves. I talked recently to a businessman whose golf game had become just as stressful as his work. He worried about his swing and lowering his handicap. He strove tensely to become more competitive, then took regular lessons to become less tense because it ruined his swing. Far from being a way of relaxing, he had made the game yet another handicap.

Most of us only know how to move in stiff straight lines, up and down, marching like soldiers on parade or moved like inanimate chess pieces. We are pawns in a game played on black and white squares. The diagonal moves of the bishop and queen are inconceivable. We can see other people being spontaneous and intimate, just living for the moment – that seems totally impossible for us. We await the instructions of the great Sergeant Major. 'Attention . . . . By the right, quick march.'

The unexpected worries and disturbs our ego. Our ego likes to be the fount of all wisdom, a know-it-all like the Delphic oracle. It manufactures it's own distinctive version of the world – a virtual reality. It likes to know what is coming next, the easier to calculate, control and manipulate. It seeks to manage our existence, to call the shots. It has learned to fear all surprises and shocks. Everything has to be understood, to fit into our preconceptions or else we might panic. There mustn't be the slightest gap. The more successful we are in controlling life and extracting all easy spontaneity, the less real life and vigour we have. As the Chinese mandarin says in the film *The Inn of the Sixth Happiness* – 'A planned life can be endured but not lived.'

One day at the Fugai Ekun monastery, the ceremonies delayed the preparation of the noon meal. When they were over the cook took up his sickle and hurriedly gathered vegetables from the garden. In his haste he lopped off part of a snake and, unaware that he had done so, threw it into the soup pot with the vegetables. Zen monks are strict vegetarians.

At the meal the monks thought they had never tasted such delicious soup, but the Roshi (head of the monastery) found something remarkable in his bowl. Summoning the cook, he held up the head of the snake and demanded, 'What is this?' The cook took the morsel, saying, 'Oh, thank you, Roshi,' and ate it'.

This cook was a consummate dancer in eating the blame – a veritable Nureyev. He could move sideways, backwards and diagonally as well as forward in straight lines. He could move with infinite speed and smoothness. Our elegant cook moves with all the fluidity of thin treacle. There is no stiffness, just suppleness, ready to move in the slightest of breezes. You can hardly see him in the middle of the dance.

The Roshi gave the cook the end of a tug of war rope and commanded him to pull. But the cook began skipping with it! Fine fellow. He could have pursued the long sad road of justification like most of us. He could have responded defensively to the Roshi's question – recrimination followed by self-justification, the old Pavlovian system. We've been through it ourselves a hundred thousand million times. 'The service was late and so I had to rush the midday meal, hence I didn't see the snake in the vegetable patch. It wasn't really my fault. Yes – I should have been more mindful, more aware . . . but you would have been the first to complain if the meal was not ready. If only I had more help in the kitchen, another two monks as assistant cooks, this kind of thing would simply not happen. . . . I know we are strict vegetarians but does it really matter, just the once? The monks really enjoyed the soup.'

There can even be dancing in our dying. Dancing in living and dancing in dying. At the moment of death we can dance with the whole of nature, to forget who we are. What stops us from dancing is fear – fear of the unknown, fear of looking stupid, fear of trivial secrets being exposed, fear of pain, fear of losing contact with others. But who or what is dying? What else is there left to do – to dance and then to die?

> *There is the story of a person who died laughing. He was a simple village person who asked a teacher the colour of Amitabha (Buddha of Compassion) that traditionally, iconographically, is red. Somehow, by mistake, he thought the teacher had said Amitabha's colour was the colour of ash in a fire. And this influenced his whole lifelong meditation practice; because when he practised visualising Amitabha, it was a grey Amitabha. Finally he lay dying and wanted to be completely sure, so he asked another teacher the colour of Amitabha. The teacher said that Amitabha's colour was red and the man suddenly burst into laughter: 'Well, I used to think him the colour of ash, and now you tell me he is red.' He burst into laughter and died laughing.* (Trungpa, 1987, p. 117).

What an absolutely marvellous way to die! Most of his earthly life spent meditating on the totally wrong colour of Amitabha. It turned out to be red rather than the colour of ash. If he ever reached Nirvana, would he ever be forgiven for his inaccurate iconography? Could Amitabha get over the affront to his colour? So what the hell! Fortunately he realised at the very moment of death the ultimate absurdity of it all. From ash colour to ashes.

As usual it takes a great Irish poet to remind us of the mixture of blossoming and dancing in ordinary living.

> *Labour is blossoming or dancing where*
> *The body is not bruised to pleasure soul,*
> *Nor beauty born out of its own despair,*
> *Nor blear-eyed wisdom out of midnight oil.*
> *O chestnut-tree, great-rooted blossomer,*
> *Are you the leaf, the blossom or the bole?*
> *O body swayed to music, O brightening glance,*
> *How can we know the dancer from the dance?*
>
> (W.B. Yeats, *Among School Children*, 1928)

Chapter 3
Temptation of Perfection

You doubt that the Divine Spark is within you. In this, you are like the others. Will you differ from them in faith which fans the spark into a brilliant fire? . . . Why are you afraid? Of what? Is it solitude or death? O strange fear! The only two things that make life bearable. (Joseph Conrad, quoted in Young, 1991, p. 17).

As we've seen, somehow we are considered just not good enough any more. The media offer a multitude of improvements on our inferior and flawed selves. There already exist vastly improved models that typify what we might become, with considerable effort and guidance from a variety of gurus and counsellors. The journey towards perfection, whatever that might mean, becomes almost irresistible. We seem increasingly under an obligation to work on ourselves, to become better. The real question is: good enough for what or for whom?

We are swamped by noisy invitations to 'improve ourselves' – to read faster, to speak more clearly – from plastic surgery to the 'working on ourselves' of the personal growth movement. More recently the growth in knowledge of genetics, has offered the even greater 'promise' of reconstructing and even adding to existing physiological structures. So we can refurbish ourselves, rid ourselves of flat feet, smelly breath, a dull personality and unruly hair. Why should living with our so obviously flawed and often damaged selves be in anyway acceptable? We can get fresh and glossy packaging so easily.

Our flaws and often charming eccentricities become increasingly patholo-gised, formally listed in the psychiatric textbooks, especially in *DSM IV* (*Diagnostic and Statistical Manual of Mental Disorders, Vol. IV*). The *DSM* system constructs diagnostic categories out of everyday living and, increasingly, behaviours that are often ordinary and even banal. Many categories like the personality disorders are vague and essentially 'untreatable'; even more bizarrely – their untreatability becomes an ingredient of their diagnosis.

Packages and ribbons
TV and magazine adverts turn us into yet another, if unusually complex, commodity in the global supermarket. We have all become easy targets for the selling of chocolate, cigarettes, cars, holidays. We all dress completely uniquely but reasonably alike – in similar T shirts, jeans, socks and trainers, carrying cloned plastic bags, all with identical fashionable logos.

We are recreated in ten thousand different images. A multitude of glossy fashion magazines tell us to look this way, to wear this colour There are powerful messages about the currently preferred sexy shapes and sizes. We are instructed about what makes us attractive, via a hundred thousand Seychelles photos. But the real media gift is to package and sell us – ourselves, all tied up with attractive ribbons. The makeover industry has entered the body, the mind and now the soul. For a brief season or two, a souped-up version of spirituality becomes popular.

Much of this is about increasing control. A former Miss Universe commented: 'For a woman to have control of her body, it's brilliant, it's empowering. Control your body and control your mind, your relationships, the rest of your life. I know that I can be any weight I want to be. How many women can say that?' (Chaudhuri, 2000, p. 6) Clearly this is a ripple of infantile omnipotence – if I control myself I can hold the universe in the palm of my elegant hand.

Magazines and newspapers, especially their colour supplements, persuade us to 'improve' – physically, socially, materially and spiritually – so they can sell us even more goods and chop down still more of the Brazilian rainforest while urging us to become 'better and more socially aware'. The trend is for articles about ecology, the greenhouse effect, global warming – whatever is sexy and fashionable. Currently there is sensible and growing pressure for more effective husbandry of the planet, campaigns against excessive waste. We have to live more prudently and wisely. These important messages are sandwiched between expensive adverts tempting us with impossibly expensive perfumes; urging us to drive bigger and faster cars guzzling ever more petrol.

But any genuine move towards better husbandry lies in robust action rather than in simply reading and listening. Action can be painful and demands a fundamental integrity. It usually means giving up cars, having one home, critically reviewing how we live and whether it's justified if it involves the use of scarce and essentially non-renewable resources. This always requires some pain and sacrifice and is founded on deep respect and reverence for this fragile planet. As the fourth-century Christian hermit, Serapion, bluntly put it: 'I have sold the book which told me to sell all I have and give the money to the poor - and given the money to the poor.'

But the real money is not in Brazilian rainforests, cleaner beaches, organic farming, respecting the planet, but in the so-called 'improvement' of 'oneself'. This is the age of mind hucksters. These psychological fitness coaches borrow from Charles Atlas and develop muscles of the mind and soul. First they need us to feel bad about ourselves. The media are full of stuff about 'pressure' and 'stress', and they increase our overall stress by devoting thousands of column inches to extolling impossible attainments, as if they were ordinary and everyday. The various remedial packages increasingly contain the magical word 'SPIRITUAL'. This is no genuine longing for liberation or enlightenment, but a crude expression of greed.

Self-improvement becomes another commodity, packaged like a breakfast cereal. 'ARE YOU WORRIED, ANXIOUS, STRESSED? Our private and personal counselling service will help you to function much more effectively.' 'COMPLETE OUR COMPREHENSIVE PERSONALITY TEST AND FIND OUT WHAT SORT OF PERSON YOU REALLY ARE.' 'Improve your personality by 100 per cent.' 'Become more effective in your approaches to MEN.' 'A thousand ways to make your MAN feel better in BED.' 'Do you really understand WOMEN?' A hundred thousand different ways of thinning our ample wallets and purses by exploring and exploiting our deepest fears and uncertainties about confidence and competence. 'If you have a social problem, we have a solution.'

Somehow we're feeling increasingly bad about ourselves. Others seem so much better. We've seen the mirror of the soul and fallen far short of vague but high standards, regularly redefined by a distant group of judges. Just as in a Kafka novel, we never get to meet these people. They keep putting up the psychological and spiritual high-jump bar, so it becomes ever harder to clear. These so-called 'experts' appear regularly in the newspapers, on television and radio. From where do they get their standards? Can they live by their own advice – have regular peak experiences, leap triumphantly over ethical walls, achieve total psychological consistency?

It's become almost immoral and a waste of our 'vast untapped potential' to be just ordinary – even normal? 'Average', 'just normal', 'very average' have become modern insults. Most of us are fairly slobbish, watch TV for long hours weekly, eat lots of food that is notably unhealthy, take insufficient exercise, and even more dreadfully obscene – smoke, take drugs and drink alcohol. So bloody what?

The struggle against personal inadequacies but not structural failings has become a war. For example disabled citizens (like me) are expected to be heroes – bravely battling against overwhelming odds, an inspiration to the rest. Complete rubbish. I don't want and don't have any need to be a hero. I am

37

firmly on the side of John Diamond, who begins his book entitled 'C – because cowards get cancer too . . .':

> *It isn't a book about a battle against cancer because I despise the set of warlike metaphors that so many apply to cancer. My antipathy to the language of battles and fights has nothing to do with pacifism and everything to do with a hatred for the sort of morality which says that only those who fight hard against their cancer survive it or deserve to survive – the corollary being that those who lose the fight deserved to do so.* Diamond, 1998, p. 10).

This attitude, which is so common in media reports, is a form of pornography.

In this context of an overall battle, ordinary vulnerability is completely unacceptable. It is repulsive and repugnant to be frightened, anxious, stupid, depressed and despairing. We must reach for the distant stars, grab a necklace of peak experiences, be 'self-actualised', at least treble our potential and turn into geniuses. We should dream (or is it more usually a nightmare) of becoming a 'better person'; more of everything our mind and grasp can desire. The heart is usually a lot wiser than that.

We desire painlessness, a sort of enduring spiritual anaesthetic, which inevitably involves an obsession with sickness and health, seen in direct opposition to health. Despair is reconfigured as clinical depression. Foucault reminds us:

> *Every society establishes a whole series of oppositions – between good and evil, permitted and prohibited, lawful and illicit, criminal and non-criminal, etc. All these oppositions, which are constitutive of society, today in Europe are being reduced to the simple opposition between normal and pathological. This opposition not only is simpler than others, but also has the advantage of letting us believe there is a technique to bring the pathological back to normal. (*Foucault, quoted in Adams, 1999, p. 58)

This results in attempts to vanquish and exclude the rejected polarity. Zero tolerance.

Yet another defence is to magic away distressed people through linguistic conjuring. The poor become 'disadvantaged' unhappy people are 'dysfunctional', battered children are transformed into 'non-accidental injuries.' The cartoonist Feiffer wrote acidly:

I used to think I was poor. Then they told me I wasn't poor, I was needy.
Then they told me it was self-defeating to think of myself as needy. I was
deprived. Then they told me that underprivileged was overused. I was
disadvantaged. I still don't have a dime. But I have a great vocabulary
(Feiffer, 1965).

Galbraith (1993, p. 97) suggests this is a strong insurance against discomfort

Those so situated, the members of the functional and socially mobilized
under class, must, in some very real way, be seen as the architects of
their own fate. If not, they could be, however marginally, on the con-
science of the comfortable. There could be a disturbing feeling,
however fleeting, of unease, even guilt. (Galbraith, 1993, p. 97)

We cannot live side by side with obviously distressed people unless they are
to blame and we are innocent. Nothing inside them or they way they live can
be allowed to disturb our lives.

This jargon of poverty and distress cleverly manipulates issues of power and
pain by transferring them to a psychological framework. Richan and
Mendelsohn (1973, p.9) comment unkindly: 'The poor have dwindled away
not in size but in presence. They have ceased to be sweating and struggling
human beings, real to the senses. For the social worker, they have been transformed into abstract entities to be studied from a distance.' One disabled
friend told me recently that two support workers had left him because they felt
over involved. When I asked what he thought they meant, he said: 'They're
supposed to be objective'.

Altruism has become especially suspect. Ideas of personal service are disparaged and derided. Those who serve others are condemned as do-gooders, out
of touch with harsh realities. Self-interest becomes the only legitimate moti-
vation, any seeming compassion is stupid or fraudulent. All of us know that's
untrue. Our daily lives are full of small moments of love, from those who
cherish us at home to strangers who politely wait while we drive into busy
lanes of traffic.

Titmuss's marvellous book on blood-giving concludes:

Practically all the voluntary donors whose answers we set down in their
own words employed a moral vocabulary to explain their reasons for
giving blood. Their view of the external world and their conception of
man's biological need for social relations could not be expressed in

*morally neutral terms. They acknowledged that they could not and should
not live entirely as they may have liked if they had paid regard solely to
their own immediate gratifications. To the philosopher's question 'what
kind of actions ought we to perform?' they replied, in effect, 'those which
will cause more good to exist in the universe than there would otherwise
be if we did not so act.'* (Titmuss ,1970, pp. 221–2).

New models

There are better quality models, just like next year's car or fridge. We're
outdated and unwanted. Now there is a 'new man', 'new woman' and even
'new child', as seen in the glossy brochures. They walk taller with more self-
assurance, are cleverer, more confident, better mentally adjusted, wittier,
handle life more effectively. They can take on all our existing roles and tasks
and conduct the London Symphony Orchestra whilst playing the mouth
organ and simultaneously composing a Shakespearean sonnet.

Of course these super individuals have their gurus – fitness coaches, personal
growth therapists, spiritual masters – to whom they pay homage. They turn
their busy lives into a business venture, never having a moment for aimless
wandering or watching Telly Tubbies. They write and illustrate coffee-table
books, produce video tapes and CDs, guiding the rest of us, all below-par
schmucks, to the fashionable Celestial City of the day in several easy steps
for only a few dollars more. With a bit of application and lots of money we
can become just like them – extremely successful, wealthy, serene and
handsome. We can join the spiritual *Baywatch* plan or become Buddhist
Bunnies, with cotton lotus blossoms covering our slim rears.

These new people are huge improvements on us; giant evolutionary steps
further on. We are Neanderthals to their Homo sapiens. They are physically
more powerful, beautiful, sexier, fitter, wiser, with an improved sense of
humour and a natural grace. They eat sensible diets, take regular exercise,
have balanced and tolerant beliefs, read improving books, listen to
Beethoven symphonies, embrace vegetarianism, subscribe to Amnesty
International and give 10 per cent of their vast incomes to Oxfam. They
never smoke, chew gum, eat cream cakes, pick their feet or noses, swear at
idiots, fart except in toilets or refuse to admit when they're wrong. They are
far beyond all sexism or racism, all forms of stigmatising and stereotyping.
They always make the right choices in relationships and would honestly level
with their intimates if things went emotionally wrong – which is never. They
work on themselves assiduously and self-consciously. Their only dreams are

about improving themselves. The one tiny problem is that they don't really exist, except as destructive fantasies inside our paranoid and fevered imaginations and profiles in the colour supplements.

The dangers lie not in fantasies about superiority but in rejection, as Foucault reminded us. For example the worship of so-called beauty necessarily involves rejection of the so-called ugly. The disabled actor Nabil Shaban (1996) invented the term 'body fascism' to describe the pernicious process of rejecting bodies that are not 'beautiful' or are seen as ugly within narrow boundaries. This rejection includes (or rather excludes!) those viewed as large, fat or elderly, and those with visible disabilities – those in wheelchairs and the vast numbers who don't look anything like Naomi Campbell or Claudia Schiffer.

Processes of exclusion are used to project dissatisfaction – a profound revulsion against the way we are, a deep and largely unattainable desire to be someone better – leading to eccentric plastic surgery, fantastic profits in cosmetics, excessive time in fitness centres. Slimming becomes a lifestyle for many women in pursuit of perfection. 'One sixth of the world's population – 800 million – have no access to health care, and the medical plight of children in many countries is getting worse' (Save the Children, 1996). This is a quest for perfection by hungry ghosts; the holy grail is no longer sought in temples, cathedrals or even Jerusalem, but hungered after in shopping malls, at Weight Watchers or growth groups, or via counselling and psychotherapy.

Shadows

We are not born ignorant but perversely forget what we know. We grow up and lose much of the intuitive understanding we gained as small children. We are carefully socialised amid an ocean of triviality and wisdom. The triviality protects us, inadequately, from a primordial fear of powerful and seemingly overwhelming shadow forces. These forces seem both separate from and hostile to us. They seem to cut the light from our life, threaten to overwhelm everything we do. They seem a perpetual enemy, of which we must be constantly vigilant. Part of our mind is constantly looking over its shoulder.

We seek distractions to avoid the shadows, squandering our preciously brief existence. This can mean almost anything – toys of all sorts, computers, hi-fi equipment, sex, cars and boats, reading books on personal growth. Usually, our main escape routes involve busyness – a thousand inconsequential activities, hurrying and scurrying rather than facing the challenge of shadowland. We read, listen to loud music, play football, watch TV and chatter on interminably, rather than face this terrifying part of ourselves, invested with our fears, despairs, hostilities and anger – profoundly unacceptable fragments of ourselves. To fail to accept those fragments, is to fail to accept the whole, and to die slowly and fearfully whilst still walking around on two legs.

We can run away from many essential realities but we can't run away from life, sickness and death. There is no escape except through suicide. We pretend that we're happy and whistle a happy tune. We learn to substitute impermanent goods and possessions for the real things in life, but moths and rust destroy them all eventually. In running away, we are forced to value the tinsel of existence. We make demands, inaccurately identified as needs. We live complicated lives that involve rushing from here to there and contain little silence and space.

In the long years of depression I could feel the shadow slowly blocking out the light; emotional light warmth fading; waking up in the morning and the great struggle to face the day. Facing also the wish to die, just not to be here – other people feeling so distant, like the freezing outer planets of Pluto or Neptune. In addition to this struggle, experiencing spinal problems so I couldn't get out of bed because of despair and paralysis. Seeing the look on people's faces, as though I'd got some contagious disease. They had to back away in case they got the virus. They exited stage right, echoing the usual duck-billed platitudes. 'You'll get better.' 'Think positive.' 'Try some tablets.'

It was far worse in the deep of the night; too scared to share with Althea, lying beside me on our lumpy futon. Unable to get to the toilet, terrified at what was happening. Losing it. My mind going round and around in a turmoil. Everything was dark and despairing. Nobody else could possibly understand.

There was a man who lived alone in a large house with a German shepherd dog. He grew afraid of it. He locked it in the dark, damp basement without food or water. It became both extremely angry and afraid. Living on the ground floor, his nights were soon disturbed by its howlings and scratchings to get out. He moved to the first floor to get away from the noise. However the following night his sleep was disturbed again as the barking grew louder, so he moved to the second floor. He slept well. The following night the barking was so loud that he moved to the attic, but he could still hear the noise of the angry dog and had nowhere else to move. He couldn't go any higher. He was both afraid and sad that he had treated his dog so badly.

So what should he do? If he opens the dank basement door suddenly, the angry and rejected dog might attack and bite him. It might feel it was under yet another attack, to be followed with further maltreatment. Becoming friends with his dog could be a slow process, establishing renewed trust and bonding. He could begin to feed and give it water through the bars of the locked door, until gradually the day comes when he can meet the dog face to face with minimal danger. In that meeting, he could begin to realise his full humanity.

Dark twins

I was visiting a 'special' psychiatric unit. It was in no way 'special', just a rubbish bin for the dangerous, bloody nuisances, human flotsam and jetsam, the complete inadequates, pretentiously labelled 'psychopaths', 'sociopaths', 'personality disorders' and other ugly terms from the psychiatric palette, meaning hardly anything, fig leaves to conceal infinite ignorance. We dump them to rot under a wafer thin layer of therapeutic compost.

I negotiated my way through the long series of electronic locks while faceless grey men and uniformed women watch me via black and white TV screens. This isn't much of a programme, hundreds of stiff visitors and staff handing over plastic cards and letters, invitations to the dance. 'Will you, won't you, will you join the dance. . . .?' But nobody quite knows the steps. Eventually we emerge deep inside the massive walls.

I am here to see Ben. He's written another scrawled letter. His case reads like a gothic novel. Small time drug pusher, petty theft, robber of sub-post offices. He was eventually convicted of buggering several children, torturing the last one with lighted cigarettes. Currently detained at her Majesty's pleasure, he's done ten years and was transferred from another unit in the far south. For everyone's peace of mind it is to be hoped that Her Majesty will have many years of pleasure.

This is our second meeting. Ben rockets off, breathlessly detailing a list of wrongs, all pencilled on the back of a used envelope. 'You've got to do something. They're abusing my rights, breaking every rule in the hospital book. First they keep my post from me for no reason. Second they confiscate my radio and portable TV and then won't let me have my *Daily Mail*. Third they're winding me up all the time, gratuitous insults – mainly from the charge nurse who really hates me.' I struggle to keep up with this tirade, scribble some notes, drawing on rusty journalist skills.

I've got such gigantically unprofessional feelings about Ben. He presses some vindictive buttons. I see him with those three children – one girl aged

43

six years and two brothers, aged seven and eight. The oldest had deep cigarette burns down his right arm and on the palm of his left hand. After more than 25 years of discipline I still experience a storming rage, but does it show through the verbiage? I can hardly look into his brown eyes as he chunters on and on. Part of me wants to scream – 'You deserve all this horrific treatment you total bastard and much worse for what you did to those children', but I remain silent. Then after a deep breath: 'Look I'll go and see the charge nurse if that's OK with you and sort something out. As you say they are clearly breaking the hospital regulations. Perhaps he'll listen to reason.' He agrees but with no great optimism.

What drives this guy? How does he live day to day with himself? One way is to get furious about injustices – those happening to him. But does he ever consider for one brief moment what he did to those children? Does he ever hear in the night their screams in his ears?

Now I'm sitting in the plastic nursing station – the ward's nerve centre, controlling 15 major miscreants and undesirables, more formally called 'criminally insane' or 'abnormal offenders'. Men who hit the newspaper headlines under words such as 'BEASTS' and 'DERANGED'. Tall, moustached charge nurse MacDonald is a neurotically difficult, thin-lipped Edinburgh Scot. We've clashed on numerous occasions. He's got Christianity badly, or rather that daily dose of constipated self-righteousness. Christ preached against his sort of Phariseeical fanaticism. I'm going with the 'High Noon' script, trying to use my rage and hostility creatively.

MacDonald preaches a perverted sermon, identifying Ben as the anti-Christ: 'This man's a complete bastard. He has turned away from redemption and embraced the temptations of sin. He's completely evil beyond the reach of God's mercy. Do you know what he did to those three young children? Do you realise how they and their good parents will suffer in the years ahead? He's got to be punished for his immense sins. I am an instrument of punishment. I will make this ward his living hell. Everyday he will experience bitter and acute misery.'

This is a truly dedicated nutcase. I'm not sure who is crazier – Ben or MacDonald. The latter is hooked on the Book of Revelations and the medieval paintings of Bosch. Ben is much brighter though less attractive. I'd rather top myself than share an arctic hut for six weeks with either. MacDonald has a manic zeal in his eyes, a stiff necked and uncircumcised look. 'High Noon' is about right.

'Funny' I said to MacDonald, 'I thought we were nurses and social workers, not priests. What's all this evil crap? Where is it in the *Nursing Times* or in the psychiatric textbooks? I thought we dealt with illness and treatment, not evil. I thought this was a hospital or at the least a prison, not a chapel. Tell me when the hospital managers decided to change their function. It's absolutely no business of ours all that religious junk. Keep it faraway from the day job. You're not employed as a priest, thank God, but as a nurse. This hospital has clear rules and you're totally violating them as part of some personal and misguided vendetta. We can go in two different ways – either very hard or very easy. The very easy way is that his post is received on a daily basis, his radio and TV are returned, he gets his *Daily Mail* every morning. The very hard way is that you do nothing but get into ignorant defiance. Then I'll make your life a complete misery. I'll bombard the senior managers with letters specifying major breaches of rules. In turn they'll persecute you, you don't get considered for promotion, you get a well-deserved reputation for troublemaking. There's absolutely no end to the mischief that I can create. I can cause so much trouble that you and your wife won't sleep at nights. I don't like Ben any more than you do. That's not the point. We've both got a job to do. Let's get on with it. You have exactly 24 hours to decide.' I rose from the chair and walked straight into the sunset – poetic licence because the autumn sun doesn't shine much over the 40-foot wall. I felt hot with energy.

Ben wrote to me after a couple of days. He had received his post and the *Daily Mail*, his radio and TV had appeared as if from nowhere. But the letter detailed further grievances. Would I visit him again? I'd liked to have seen MacDonald playing Santa Claus. Of course they're both serious lunatics. One has professional training and is paid, the other has neither. One is emotionally constipated, consumed with self-righteous: the other has sour and vicious memories of violating small children and the giant shadows of a hellish childhood.

Ben probably has more insight. They feed off each other, and perhaps more worryingly I need both. They live together on a daily institutional basis and I'm the complete stranger in town, Clint Eastwood's pale rider. It's the common story of sheriffs and outlaws, advocates and service professionals. Can one survive without the other? Can either survive without the stranger redefining the balance of power until the next time? This triangle of roles – rescuer, victim, oppressor – is really powerful. But who is playing which role?

Losers and winners

We are obsessive about measuring our 'achievements'. Socially and economically we play 'winners and losers'. Losers are on the dole or have poorly paid or worthless jobs. They live in run-down council house estates, probably in northern England, Scotland or Wales. They eat fried bread, beefburgers, fish and chips, and are labelled 'malingerers' by the popular media. They are on the far edges of our society. They share most of the sorrows and very few of the joys.

Take this extract from an editorial about Romanian gypsies in the *Sun* newspaper (14 March 2000) as just one of many examples:

BENEFIT CONS BEGGAR BELIEF
When the Sun and its readers protest that asylum seekers are making mugs of us, the chattering classes have a standard response. 'You're prejudiced because you're ignorant of the facts.' . . . The beggars are taking us for a ride. They earn more in an hour's begging on the streets of London than the average Romanian makes in a week. And they are using it – and their social security which is paid for by YOUR taxes – to build marble palaces for the rest of the scroungers back home.

Winners are valued and 'successful', acquiring the mountain of consumer durables that proclaim their 'high' social status. For a brief moment they can deceive themselves, feel at the top of the pecking order, the king or queen of the cardboard castle. They can show the world their large country estate, motor launch, Rolls Royce or platinum American Express card. But these 'successful' people really know that an accumulation of material possessions is no genuine achievement. What particular merit has a shroud with golden threads? From the *Tao Te Ching*:

> *The greatest achievement seems like falling short,*
> *but its effects are beyond measure.*
> *Being filled up feels like being emptied out,*
> *But never like running dry.*

(Freke, 1995, p. 87)

The vital realities of our lives – such as being born, our dependence on others, becoming sick, dying and death – are denied and almost completely submerged under a hogwash of external activity. We are packaged and sanitised. We are hopelessly lost in the noisy global market. That is an immense cost for a few hours of escape from fear.

Matt Seaton, husband of Ruth Picardie, illustrates this struggle when watching his wife dying over the months.

> *You always imagine death as a sudden event, a clean break between being and non-being, possession and loss – and for some facing perhaps the dreadful trauma of losing a loved one killed suddenly in an accident, that is how it must be. But with a progressive disease like cancer, dying is a relentlessly attritional process of estrangement. You want so much to do and say the right thing, but you are doomed to frustration, failure and regret. The only really 'right thing' would be to make that person you love well again, and that is the one great godlike task you cannot perform.* (Picardie, 1998, p. 103)

The dying of a loved one shatters all social conventions. Ordinarily we feel compelled to wear a social face, a smoothly smiling face that is acceptable, likeable and popular but without authenticity. Who are we? We have forgotten how to communicate with others. We have sold our integrity for some cheap social acceptability. We translate our natural changeability into a learned consistency with little substance. This face buys shallow acceptance. To be rejected might mean social death, perhaps to be viewed as mad. To be deemed crazy, psychotic, the 'odd one out' or as 'making waves' is a fundamental fear. Events such as dying and death crash through all of that skin-deep presentation.

The more successful the social presentation, the more lonely we become. We are on our own even in the presence of many others, no matter how intimate. John Clare, the nineteenth-century lunatic poet, wrote of living with the 'shipwreck of my own esteem.' (Clare, 1996, p. 107) As young children, we knew loneliness as an occasional visitor, especially at night. Now that visitor has taken up lodgings. Our essential selves are brick-walled from others. We can never show our real and essentially vulnerable selves. We can show only the tidy ends, the authentic untidiness remains closely concealed.

> *'Many people fear nothing more terribly than to take a position which stands out sharply and clearly from the prevailing opinion. The tendency of most of us is to take a position that is so ambiguous that it will include everything and so popular that it will include everyone.' (Martin Luther King Junior).*

But that means denying our human uniqueness, all the personal experiences and true feelings – ultimately to bury the deep knowledge of who we really are.

Now we live hand to mouth – often frightened, joyful, anxious, angry, loving, untidy, feeling ugly and unwanted – we begin to feel less real than the people in a breakfast cereal TV advert, with glowing faces and eager anticipation of the day ahead. Everyone else seems so much more alive. We watch ourselves like thousands of football spectators. Our minds are fragmented much of the time. There are more post mortems than real action. Even when we feel good, we know that further bouts of despair and self-doubt are just around the corner.

News items with films of bombings in Chechnya, floods in Mozambique, earthquakes in Japan – these come from another planet. We watch starving, bloated babies somewhere in Africa or South America – these are a pervasive reality and yet TV adverts frequently seem more relevant and real. We are stockaded, but not effectively, against the fundamental brutality of the world.

Temptations

There is a great temptation to see spirituality as something special, involving superior powers. It is usually written of as if it contains extra ingredients that are possessed only by the chosen few – modern Calvinism. '[O]ne of the ways in which "spirit" has been interpreted is to separate it altogether from organised religion and a set of beliefs and link it to a "special way of being". Spirit and spiritual states are seen as something beyond the mundane and everyday.' (Petrioni, 1993, ch. 33) This sort of quest for perfection is destructive, whether in chocolate cakes or in gurus.

This Disneylike process – the temptation to beautify and sentimentalise, concentrating exclusively on light rather than darkness – is powerful and injurious.

> *As a finite self, then, a human struggles to find goodness, truth, beauty and life at the exclusion of evil, falsity, ugliness and death. But such one-sided fulfilment is impossible. Given the inseparability of the poles, one cannot arrive at a pure or absolute form of one pole at the exclusion of the other. Although someone might find temporary, relative satisfaction, the negation of that satisfaction soon arises. Expressed with the metaphor of waves, insofar as people exist as waves on the agitated surface of an expanse of water, they are eternally unsettled, for waves continue to arise and fall in endless opposition.* (Ives, 1992, p. 74)

New age guru was age old hypocrite

Inevitably and with monotonous regularity, it's revealed that our favourite spiritual gurus chewed tobacco, drank excessively, or were fond of sex with beautiful men and women. My *Guardian* newspaper tells me rather late in the day that Kahlil Gibran, author of the classic, best-selling book *The Prophet* was a womaniser and an alcoholic (Millar, 1998, p. 5) A difficult combination I should imagine.

Why do spiritual teachers have to be perfect? The worship of any sort of idol, false or genuine, is both dangerous and destructive. The Zen masters and Tibetan lamas I've known were ordinary men and women shrouded in projected mystery, capable of great heights and extraordinary stupidities. My first Zen teacher asked through a cloud of cigarette smoke: 'David – you'd prefer it if I didn't smoke?' I nodded vigorously and affirmatively. She responded just as quickly: 'Bad luck.' It was a profound teaching. She was relaying the essential truth of Orwell's remark about Gandhi: 'No doubt alcohol, tobacco and so forth are things that a saint must avoid, but sainthood is also a thing that human beings must avoid'. (Lomas, 1987, p. 12)

It is easy to get absurdly fluffy about spirituality. The paradoxes become filled with mystical nonsense. Much of what passes for contemporary spirituality is linked with the New Age movement, characterised by promiscuity – the borrowing and stealing from hundreds of different disciplines. This results in an unhealthy sprint from reason, taking refuge in a mess of sentimentality and hugging – the widespread public grieving for Princess Diana is one excellent example. Our yearning for spirituality can invent other commodities, all improved products with fresh ingredients.

This problem is not at all new. Hooker, the sixteenth-century preacher, commented:

> *Hence an error groweth, when men in heaviness of spirit suppose they lack faith, because they find not the sugared joy and delight which indeed doth accompany faith, but so as a separable accident, as a thing that may be removed from it; yea there is a cause why it should be removed. The light would never be acceptable, were it not for that usual intercourse of darkness. Too much honey doth turn to gall; and too much joy even spiritually would make us wantons. Happier a great deal is that man's case, whose soul by inward desolation is humbled, than he whose heart is through abundance of spiritual delight lifted up and exalted above measure.* (Keble, 1845, pp 474–5).

Spiritual gifts are easily used for egotistical purposes, subverting even the noblest of intentions. Sawaki Roshi comments brusquely:

to do good can be bad. There are people who do good deeds to adorn themselves. . . . Everything turns on whether one believes in religion in order to improve oneself or whether one lets go of the mind that wants to gain something. The former is a heretic who exploits God and the Buddha, and the latter is a truly religious person. (Uchiyama, 1990, pp. 67-8)

To Buddhists, spirituality is a journey and about melting barriers:

that one is all things: mountains, rivers, grasses, trees, sun, moon, stars, universe, are all oneself... Realising this naturally results in what we commonly refer to in Zen Buddhism as 'true compassion'. Other people and things are no longer seen as apart from oneself, but on the contrary, as one's own body. (Genpo, quoted in Brandon, 1985b pp. 4–5)

This is the essential harmony of ordinary everyday living rather than devotion to self-cherishing.

Trungpa, the Tibetan lama, rightly warned against the dangers of self-improvement.

It means that whatever we do with our practice, if that practice is connected with our personal achievement, which is called 'spiritual materialism,' or the individual glory that we are in the right and others are wrong, and we would like to conquer their wrongness or evil because we are on the side of God and so forth – that kind of bullshit or cow dung is regarded as eating poisonous food. Such food may be presented to us beautifully and nicely, but when we begin to eat it, it stinks. (Trungpa, 1993, p. 178)

We need to care more about the so-called good intentions than about so-called bad ones. Most of us have damaged someone we loved, through forms of 'idiot compassion' – caring that comes from our own needs rather than from genuine empathy for the other.

Simpler still is the emphasis on one's own competence at the expense of the other. 'Thus according to the Rabbi of GER, the single most important issue in the rabbi – client relationship is how the rabbi deals with the potential for arrogance when people come to him for answers and he resists the temptation to 'rattle them off', so as to speak, to the client.' (Polsky and Wozner, 1989, p. 78) This is yet another aspect of the Icarus Syndrome. Our own wisdom and competence is stressed at the expense of others. As Cicero wrote: 'The authority of those who teach is very often a hindrance to those who wish to learn' (Montaigne, 1958, p. 53)

Real heroes

Wise Odysseus rejected the apparent magic of immortality, of attaining perfection in Homer's *Odyssey*. The goddess Calypso, who saved his life and
tended him for seven years, entreats him not to leave for Ithaca, where his
wife Penelope awaits. Odysseus responds with consummate diplomacy:

> *My lady goddess, do not be angry at what I am about to say. I too know
> well enough that my wise Penelope's looks and stature are insignificant
> compared with yours. For she is mortal, while you have immortality and
> unfading youth. Nevertheless I long to reach my home and see the day of
> my return. It is my never-failing wish. And what if one of the gods does
> wreck me on the wine-dark sea? I have a heart that is inured to suffering
> and I shall steel it to endure that too. For in my day I have had many
> bitter and painful experiences in war and on the stormy seas. So let this
> disaster come. It only makes one more.* (Homer's, *Illiad*).

He rejects the certainty of enduring love and immortality in the arms of the
never fading Calypso. He chooses the unique human heritage – the ordinary
life of a Greek hero, triumphs and disasters, illness and eventual death. In our
contemporary terms, in the age of plastic surgery, the dawn of cloning and
the growth of ten thousand psychological tricks, he gives up perfection for
ordinary human living.

He has arrived at a genuine understanding of imperfections. He doesn't want
to eradicate them – but to learn and grow from their promptings.

> *Why do you want to shut out of your life any agitation, any pain, any
> melancholy, since you really do not know what these states are
> working upon you? Why do you want to persecute yourself with the
> question whence all this may be coming and whither it may be bound?
> If there is anything morbid in your processes, just remember that
> sickness is the means by which an organism frees itself of foreign
> matter; so one must help it to be sick, to have its whole sickness, and
> break out with it, for that is its purpose* (Rilke, 1954).

The poet Rilke writes of eradication; the extermination of the unwanted and
reviled. We want to get rid of physical noise – stopping us from getting on
with whatever we've decided our life is about. Our existing government uses
zero tolerance as a way of dealing with complex social issues, connected to us
all. At present the newspapers are full of stuff about zero tolerance to beggars.
London police are extending their policy of arresting beggars – especially

those considered aggressive. The Victorian debate about the deserving and undeserving poor has never really gone away. We are in great danger of using ideological aerosol sprays on difficult and extremely complex social issues. 'Exterminate, exterminate, exterminate' cried Dr Who's Daleks. We are zapping the beggars and moving them off the streets, to where? We demand speedy and effective remedies, rather than trying to understand how we are all interlinked and why it is undesirable to have the sort of life we wish.

We have to give up this war against ourselves; the unceasing struggle against our ordinariness and grasping for the extraordinary, thinly concealed under the skin of personal growth. There is nothing fundamentally wrong with the way we are. In Thich Nhat Hanh's terms we have many true names.

> *I am the child in Uganda, all skin and bones,*
> *my legs as thin as bamboo sticks,*
> *and I am the arms merchant, selling deadly weapons to Uganda.*
> *I am the twelve-year-old-girl, refugee on a small boat,*
> *who throws herself into the ocean after being raped by the sea pirate,*
> *and I am the pirate, my heart not yet capable of seeing and loving.*
> *I am a member of the politburo, with plenty of power in my hands,*
> *and I am the man who has to pay his 'debt of blood' to my people,*
> *dying slowly in a forced labour camp.*
> *My joy is like spring, so warm it makes flowers bloom in all walks of life.*
> *My pain is like a river of tears, so full it fills all four oceans.*
> *Please call me by my true names, so I can hear*
> *all my cries and laughs at once,*
> *so I can see that my joy and pain are one.*
> *Please call me by my true names, so I can wake*
> *up and so the door of my heart can be left open,*
> *the door of compassion.*

(Hanh, 1982, p. 63-4)

We are the homeless people in the night shelter next door; the social service bureaucrats as well as residential workers supporting people with disabilities; we nurse the patients – sick and dying in hospital – as well as sell military hardware to the Middle East and patent for profit the discoveries of human DNA research. We are all of us so much more than lengthy lists of problems, symptoms and diseases. We are a huge and necessary diversity of peoples and individuals, each one a galaxy of elements.

We must strongly resist reductions in diversity, especially when it happens, either directly or indirectly, because of our own activities. It needs a profound celebration and reverence. We are part of a world where the total number of species is rapidly declining, in biological terms – the opposite to progress. There are only 2–300 Right whales left in the North Atlantic ocean. The palaeontologist Gould (1994, p.286) comments: 'Our vaunted ladder of progress is really the record of declining diversity in an unsuccessful lineage that then happened upon a quirky invention called consciousness.'

That passage echoes love and joy and contrasts immensely with DSM IV mentioned earlier, squashing people into tiny boxes. There is enormous pressure to be similar; to fit in, to believe the same ideas, wear the same things or risk exclusion, to become invisible. Gould and Darwin's biological magnificence is found in and amongst us, the miraculous diversity of sex, gender, race, skin colour, height and breadth, and varying ideas and aspirations.

In a more recent book Gould (1996, p.29) begs us to give up this illusion of progress. 'We crave progress as our best hope for retaining human arrogance in an evolutionary world.' After Galileo, Einstein and even Freud, we try to hang onto a pathetic sort of significance on this planet and in this universe, that we are in some way more special than anything else. Our supreme arrogance that in some way the world was created for us has neither scientific nor spiritual reality.

Chapter 4
Vulnerability as Strength

In the world there is nothing more submissive and weak than water.
Yet for attacking that which is hard and strong nothing can surpass it.
This is because there is nothing that can take its place.
That the weak overcomes the strong,
And the submissive overcomes the hard,
Everyone in the world knows yet no one
can put this knowledge into practice.

(Lau, 1963, p.140)

As we've seen, we are constantly exhorted to be more competent and less vulnerable. We strive to learn much more and to become muscular in physical, psychological and spiritual senses. In contrast the *Tao Te Ching* reminds us of the strength and wisdom of vulnerability. 'That the weak overcomes the strong.' This leads us on to Shamanism – healing through wounds. How can we learn to accept these immense treasures inside us and use them for the benefit of all? What sort of training would be necessary?

The overvaluing of competence can mean hiding the 'unacceptable' bits from ourselves and others. Kay Jamison, a professor of psychiatry and a psychiatric patient writes:

I am tired of hiding, tired of misspent and knotted energies, tired of the hypocrisy, and tired of acting as though I have something to hide. One is what one is, and the dishonesty of hiding behind a degree, or a title, or any manner and collection of words, is still exactly that: dishonest. Necessary, perhaps but dishonest. I continue to have concerns about my decision to be public about my illness, but one of the advantages of having had manic-depressive illness for more than thirty years is that very little seems insurmountably difficult. (Jamison, 1995b, pp. 7–8)

We can use these experiences of distress and isolation to enter other worlds. They can help narrow the boundaries between different sorts of reality, enlarging our experience and bringing us into more intimate and direct contact with loving others. A healing that means melting the boundaries, being less partial to ourselves and creatively including others in more intimate and wholesome ways. Our broken hearts can make us more available to others.

Withering?

Direct experience becomes gradually devalued and even rejected. The suffering and poverty of the vast majority turns into yet another service industry. Antidiscrimination strategies become ends in themselves, just mantras for use in college student assignments, separated from any genuine struggle against racism or sexism. We lose sight of the overall struggle for liberation. Walsh (1990, p.160) comments:

> *a tradition no longer focuses on or even appreciates direct experience of the transcendent. Then what is left is an institution largely devoid of direct experience of the sacred... Techniques for inducing altered states then give way to mere symbolic rituals, direct experience is replaced by belief, and living doctrine fossilizes into dogma.*

What remains is simply a series of empty rituals.

These suffocating trends have enormous consequences for health and social services in stimulating a culture of fear and competition. Diverse professions compete aggressively with each other, to achieve dominance – nursing versus social work, psychology versus psychiatry. . . . Their very survival seems to depend on the destruction or at the very least the diminution of the other, rather than in making vital connections to expand common knowledge. Reports about scandal after scandal make important points about the failure of the mental health services to cooperate fully, to save the life of a child or prevent patients from killing themselves.

One disturbing tendency is to industrialise human helping. As we saw with *DSM* labelling, differentness can easily become understood as deficiency. Human needs father a business more closely linked to professional ambitions than any needs of the distressed service users. People are encouraged to become the passive recipients of quasimonopolistic services; to be a cash crop for exploitation. Vast tensions in socioeconomic structures are reframed as in some way the fault of individual 'consumers'.

Ironically, major socioeconomic changes select ever more groups for social exclusion and then have to provide the relevant professionals to herd them – social workers, nurses, occupational therapists. Wilkinson (1996, p.171) writes of the 'unrelenting processes of social differentiation which reflect and amplify social hierarchy. . . . It is these processes which create social exclusion, which stigmatise the most deprived and establish social distances throughout society.' Such devalued individuals pay extremely high costs.

These powerful trends are an essential ingredient of the 'consumer' revolution. We gradually leave behind ways of living, understood as a series of actions for yet another that is simply a collection of experiences – more passive than active – from being heroic to sunbathing on a sandy beach.

> *Tourists, holidaymakers, and others are not doing anything very much: they are simply purchasing and laying down stocks of pleasant memories to be replayed and enjoyed in later years. People are not agents any longer; they are the consumers and the recorders of their own experience. They are their own video-librarians, collecting and arranging shelves of happy memories.'* (Cupitt, 1998, p. 15)

Actions are replaced by holiday scrapbooks.

Consumers demand services that are easier to access. Everything from education upwards and downwards must be glycerined. Kenyon (1997, p.25) writes:

> *The fact is that Brahms needs effort, not just on the part of the performer but from the listener. And we underestimate that at our peril. The big classical works – not just the huge symphonies of Bruckner and Mahler and the operas of Wagner, but also Handel operas, Bach cantatas – make demands on the listener just as do a great book or a great picture.*

This sort of challenge lies uneasily with the wishes of consumers for smooth products that ask for little effort.

Icarus syndrome
It was very many years ago but it remains fresh in my memory. I wanted to train for professional social work so attended a selection interview for the course at Sussex University. I'd been a senior mental welfare officer for several years, written the required essay on family background – poverty in Sunderland, regular physical battering accompanied with torrents of sarcasm from my Dad, running away from home, homelessness in London.

The academic tutor was an earnest intellectual with a degree of studied, 'objective' distance that I found disconcerting. He was not at all empathic, rather grim. The hour-long interview felt like an incessant prodding by a long pole. Right at the end he leaned over and remarked languidly: 'Of course with your background, if we accepted you, we would insist on psychiatric treatment. How would you feel about that?'

'Psychiatric treatment. . . .' Struggling to answer I felt battered again. Instantly I was demoted from senior lunatic catcher to junior lunatic. The insistence on psychiatric treatment was made with rubber gloves. I gathered myself together, or rather made a pale imitation of it and muttered 'OK'. It was far from convincing. I'd received a valuable social work lesson. Until that moment it had never occurred to me that my Durham childhood was a 'problem'. But the Pandora's Box was opened, never to be closed again.

The damaged and wounded side of me has seemed, for the most part, unacceptable to my chosen profession. I've written widely about being battered; appeared on prime-time TV shows to talk about the beatings; even made training films on violence. Professionally the response has been largely hostile. Modern social workers are not supposed to be 'damaged goods'. Now we're all managers and technicians, not teachers or healers. Few articles in the journals acknowledge the hidden reasons why many people come to the 'helping professions'. These have much to do with expiation, guilt, seeking forgiveness, experiencing loneliness. This profession was founded on the wounds and scars of people with experiences like mine. We have grown fat and influential on the suffering of neglected and damaged children. We have created a whole new industry out of their pain.

Icarus was the son of Daedalus who made waxen wings to escape from Minos and the island of Crete.

> *Icarus disobeyed his father's instructions and began soaring towards the sun, rejoiced by the lift of his great sweeping wings. Presently, when Daedalus looked over his shoulder, he could no longer see Icarus; but scattered feathers floated on the waves below. The heat of the sun had melted the wax, and Icarus had fallen into the sea and drowned. (Graves, 1955, p. 88)*

His pride in his own performance resulted in sudden death in the sea.

Olshansky (1972) writes:

> *First, professionals, by training, are committed to treating pathology and abnormality even where none exists. . . . Second, professionals too often develop a sense of superiority to the people they help. Enjoying feelings of superiority, they somehow lose interest and faith in the capacity of their 'inferiors' to change, to grow. Moreover, they expect less from these 'inferior' persons. Third, professionals tend to see . . . only the 'inner space', the intrapsychic . . . professionals tend to place*

*a low value on experience. The only experiences they value are the
clinical ones, where they are in control and their contacts are brief. The
experiences outside the clinic seem to them to be of little value . . . .
Fourth, professionals are imprisoned by habits. They prefer to do what
they have done. It is easier and more comfortable to treat pathology as
they have been doing and as they have been trained to do.*

The other side of this issue, is the pressure from patients and clients for us to
become gods. We demand that doctors don't make mistakes, always get it
right. The *British Medical Journal* has described doctors as 'the second
victim of medical error', often paying for a mistake with their mental health,
marriages and livelihood. 'The easy, understandable and completely wrong
answer is to blame those who made the mistake' (Rice, 2000, p. 25). So the
next time some medic saws the wrong leg off, meditate on their structural
problems! The *British Medical Journal* has understandably come up with
the completely wrong answer – to erase large zones of personal and professional responsibility.

Much of this adds up to a flight from pain, a protection against getting too
close to emotional and psychological distress, the development of yet more
rituals. When doing field social work I had a file allocated to me. It contained
a query about the possible battering of an old lady by a relative. Seven social
workers had visited over a number of years. Periodically at a local day centre,
the old lady was seen to have bruises on her legs and upper arms. On a number
of occasions this was referred to the social work team and investigated.
Nothing was discovered about these bruises.

I visited on two occasions. On the second occasion the male relative broke
down in floods of tears and 'confessed' to ill-treating his elderly relative. He
had in his own words been 'wanting to clear things up for some time'. He felt
that the various professionals concerned 'didn't wish to hear about the
violence'. They were looking at him 'through plate glass'.

These sorts of defensive strategies serve as a barrier. It often seems to us as
professionals that accidents and illness, dying and death, divorce and sorrow
are processes happening to others – not to us. Working with others can be a
sort of voyeurism, spectator therapy. I recall seeing a patient who was also a
social worker, specialising in marital breakdown. A few months earlier her
husband had left her for a young woman. She couldn't understand why it was
such a dire struggle. 'I've been through so many breakdowns.' But this time
it was a direct experience, not one to be listened to and watched.

At another level, sickness, especially that with a high psychological component, becomes a fresh sort of immorality, involving the unforgivable burdens placed on others. My wife got cancer a few years ago and nowadays avoids reading anything about it. Most writings make her feel guilty. She feels blamed by much of the sensational output from radio, TV and in magazines and newspapers. If only she'd ridden twenty miles a day on a monocycle, eaten two kilograms of raw rhubarb weekly, washed it down with a quart of pure halibut oil whilst listening to relaxation tapes. The more guilty she feels, the more stress and that is linked with cancer.

I struggled for several years with spinal problems and wrote a diary.

I've had several years of tremendous back pain. Other people have back troubles but nothing like mine. I've sobbed myself to sleep with it, many a night. Never mind the 'big boys don't cry' crap, this one does and often. It is a prolapsed disc problem linked with curvature of the spine. Nowhere and no position has any comfort. Ordinary walking is agony. I lie down rather than sit. It is chronic and exhausting misery, impossible to rest even by sleeping. I keep painfully turning over and over, trying to find some relief. It preoccupies my waking hours.

I searched for healers. They had rituals and white coats, leather couches, usually freezing hands; communicated solemnly amid the frequent purification of hand washings. Mostly they subtly deprecated the last professional I'd attended. When I described the previous interventions there was a slight lifting of eyebrows and increased tension round the mouth. The implication was usually that I was an idiot who'd entirely neglected himself and had put himself foolishly in the cold hands of other barely qualified idiots.

They were talented at communicating disapproval. I was somehow to blame. Diamond describes a particular cul-de-sac when writing about surviving cancer:

It seems that there is a small space where new age philosophy meets sharp-heeled Thatcherism and it is in the idea that we are all entirely responsible for our individual physical states. In a way, of course, that is true enough: my choice to smoke for all those years, to live in the centre of our smokiest city, to eat full English breakfasts in bad provincial hotels must certainly have taken its toil on heart and artery and bronchial tube.

And yes, if I still smoked and carried on doing so through the treatment I would accept that I may bear the responsibility for the cure not working. It's the idea of taking spiritual responsibility for a disease once it's been diagnosed which annoys me. For it leads to the idea of the survivor as personal hero – that only those who want to survive enough get through to the end, and the implied corollary that those who die are somehow lacking in moral fibre and the will to live.

I'll accept that some can grit their teeth, and get through the treatments more happily than others, and even that there are various calming regimes which make the treatment slightly more bearable. In terms of responsibility, though, as far as I'm concerned I will be cured only if the surgeons have cut out the right bits of my neck and the radiologists and radiographers have chosen the right bits of my throat to point their machine at. (Diamond, 1998, p. 196–7)

This sharply observed position is underpinned by an acute lack of humility on the part of New Age healers, a tendency not unknown in mainstream medicine. This is a fresh sort of fascism. My spinal experiences were that surgery and physiotherapy didn't help much, neither did crystal swinging or the laying on of hands. What helped was swimming and taking responsibility, not culpability, for the distress. For 18 months I was the first person to arrive each morning at 7 am at Preston swimming baths. At the end I still disliked swimming but my back was much stronger.

Kavan

I've long since given up playing at Icarus – well most of the time. Kavan is a very effective spiritual teacher. It's lunchtime, but as I'm on this draconian diet to shift a sagging stomach my plate is empty. I'm making a meal at very short notice for Kavan, a large friend who has physical disabilities. One of his personal assistants dropped out at short notice for sketchy reasons. I am struggling to heat a prepared dish of minced beef and pasta which, as I am a vegetarian, is a considerable sacrifice of principle.

I am fuming inside. A well-known professor of community care with more than 170 published works to his credit, is making lunch for a man with a disability whilst a dozen research projects await. As recompense I gain large numbers of brownie points and gold stars. I am far away from the imagined ivory towers inhabited by academics. I am working at the coal face in the real world where it's all happening, whilst other social work tutors, god help them, bend arthritically over computers and move mountains of paper from one side of their desks to the other in between attending interminable meetings.

Kavan keeps asking: 'Who was supposed to do my lunch? Who has dropped out? I am unhappy about this.' He's unhappy! What about me? Dragged away at five minutes' notice from my office and struggling with a dumb microwave. I take his lunch to the tray on the wheelchair for the third time. 'It's still cold' he grimaces. Whatever my limited skills as a social work teacher, I'm useless as a cook. These banal practicalities are the real test, not the ability to write books or research.

For the seventh time: 'Who should be doing my lunch?' I don't know or care one bit. Anyone except me. Boringly he tells me once more that he's unhappy. I know he's unhappy. I struggle again with the microwave, having just failed to find any potatoes. Kavan has a marvellously subtle way of requesting something and when you can't comply he responds with an implication of incompetence, honed over many years in residential care. The potatoes must be there, it's just that I'm too stupid to see them.

I'm now chock full of rage. I'm so angry with him because he asks the same question over and over again to which I don't know the answer. I know about memory loss due to the head injury. I'm beginning to feel that I should know who dropped out. My anger rattles around the cutlery drawer. Now I can't find anything even the napkins. Kavan asks very pointedly how I became a professor. He seems bemused rather than fascinated. It obviously didn't include microwave oven or potato tests as I take his meal out once more and simultaneously explain about the obligatory oral exam – for the professorship not the cooking.

He's deeply angry too – stuck in that bloody wheelchair while the real world goes by. From the promise of a young soldier, playing prop forward for the Cheshire rugby union team to life in a wheelchair, seldom going out. Planned routines, an important aspect of his everyday life, are disregarded by thoughtless others. Waiting all day for a social worker, who never comes because she's too busy. Sacred staffing rotas are ignored and unexpected professors are dumped on you, and even the microwave mounts a dumb resistance.

I know a thousand clever tricks from psychotherapy training and social work to process and juggle this anger. I can envision pink flamingos flying over the African plains; hear light waltz music to relax tense tissues; do yoga asanas on my neck; punish myself with an ideological birch for falling short of the 150 social work lunch preparation competencies – from empathy to communication skills.

I choose none of the above. The immense anger surges up my body almost to choking point. After a brief period of this surge, I can feel Kavan's frustration every time he speaks, both in overtones and in undertones. Some comes from immense disappointment about life in a wheelchair, having to depend on frequently unreliable people making your lunch, whilst mine comes from a childhood of poverty and Dad daily beating me up.

'Would you like some peas?' I ask. I can find a packet of peas but no potatoes. 'Yes' he responds like a demented parrot, 'But who was supposed to do my lunch? Where are they? I'm unhappy.' For the umpteenth time I respond that I don't know. I wish I did know. It's an extremely large part of the human condition to be unhappy. It arises out of the great disappointment that life isn't the way it ought to be, but is the way it is. The person supposed to prepare the lunch didn't show up; didn't care enough; didn't follow the script of the rota. Kavan and I share that disappointment in spades, except that my begrudging generosity is to be punished, instead of the bastard who sloped off somewhere. It's the story of my life. Who are we and who is unhappy?

When I've finished all these ideological ramblings, simply a major distraction, there's still lunch to get. The damned microwave is infuriating. None of the buttons work. Why do machines always make me feel stupid? He's hungry and so am I. Spin-dryer mind whirls round and round again. Anger; healthy eating or rather not eating; accumulating lots of brownie points; unhappiness; should be somewhere else; deep disappointment about not being a good enough person; should feel warm compassion for Kavan but don't at present; return reluctantly to the discipline of mindful practice; come back to the kitchen and attend to the lunch. This time the minced beef and veg meets the Kavan test, but only just. 'Can I have some more coffee?' I make the coffee ungraciously, and then there's all the washing up.

> *The Great Way is not difficult*
> *for those who don't pick or choose.*
> *When love and hate are both absent*
> *everything becomes clear and undistinguished.*
> *Make the smallest distinction, however*
> *and heaven and earth are set infinitely apart.'*
> *If you wish to see the truth*
> *then hold no opinions for or against anything.*
> (Sengstan, 'Hsin Hsin Ming', in Brandon, 1985b, p. 8)

I wonder what that dreadful old Zen monk Sengstan, far back in sixth-century China, meant by all that pious rubbish!

Wounds

The book *Wounded Healers* (Rippere and Williams, 1985) contains accounts by professionals who have suffered from depression, including psychiatrists, nurses and social workers. After their breakdowns they encountered three kinds of reaction from colleagues: *active support* – accepting them, assuring them that their job was safe: 'You're O.K. We still want to know you'; *apparent indifference* – not noticing their distress or depression, making no comment: *overt hostility* – employers trying to get rid of them and hostile receptions from colleagues.

In recovery, most felt their skills and empathy had been improved by the experience. A 'fallen' social worker wrote: 'Looking back on my period of depression, I feel it was a turning point in my life. It threw me back on my own resources, and although this was enormously painful at the time, it was the beginning of a long process during which I began to discover what I wanted for myself as an individual rather than as a wife.' (ibid. p. 93)

That is in stark contrast with this vision of practice in a best-selling social work textbook:

> *For most people, most of the time, the human way of life ensures self-maintenance; but for a minority, either because of defects of birth, deprivation during childhood, the onset of sickness and old age, the experience of an accident, the shock of bereavement or job loss, or the ill-effects of political, economic or social planning or discrimination, self-sufficiency runs out, and the need for a maintenance mechanic becomes apparent. This need pinpoints the heart of the social worker's role.* (Davies, 1985)

The essential tools are spanners and a handbook – not much space for the healing potential of wounds!

All of us are damaged and wounded. The challenge is to use these wounds in the compassionate service of others. Our so-called defects are an important way to serve others. There is an old story of a middle-aged Japanese woman, as sharp as a lemon. She had brought up her only son after her husband died suddenly of a heart attack. She had become embittered; felt that life had dealt unfairly with her. She worked hard, cleaning and washing for a living for little reward.

When the son was nearly 18, the headmaster called to see her. He was highly respected as a teacher but nationally known as a calligrapher. 'Your son is very talented. He should go to university and enter a profession. I know you have little money but, with your permission, I could write a letter of introduction to the Dean of the faculty at Kyoto University, whom I know from university days. He might decide to take him and find a bursary.' The mother accepted and watched the headmaster take out a piece of paper and write the letter with a blunt pencil borrowed from her. She was puzzled that he didn't use his brushes and pens and inks. A few weeks later she travelled with her son to the university.

After handing in the letter to the Dean's secretary, they waited in the corridor. The Dean came to collect them and was very friendly. He explained that his respect for his old colleague – the headmaster, was so great that he was willing to take the son. 'Over the next few days, I will try to find a bursary and a place for your son to live. I have just one request. Is it possible that I can have this letter because it's a work of art and I should like to frame it?' She explained that the letter belonged to him and then travelled back home alone.

Over the next few days she was both sad and joyful. She reflected on the blunt pencil. It made no real sense when he had such excellent pens and brushes. Then she awakened. She was herself a blunt pencil – self-pitying, nothing special, but in the hands of a master, giving herself over to the Lord Buddha – she could be a vehicle for the creation of a work of art. Most of us are blunt pencils, some – like me – perhaps much too blunt for this increasingly sophisticated world. In the right hands, gradually giving up our demands and bitterness, we can be used to create masterpieces, worthy of framing.

Wonders
Wordsworth's writing often echoed a wholesome wonder, a respect and worship, detecting an underlying presence:

> *And I have felt*
> *A presence that disturbs me with the joy*
> *Of elevated thoughts; a sense sublime*
> *Of something far more deeply interfused,*
> *Whose dwelling is the light of setting suns,*
> *And the round ocean and the living air,*
> *And the blue sky, and in the mind of man:*
> *A motion and a spirit that impels*
> *All thinking things, all objects of all thought,*
> *And rolls through all things.*
>
> (Wordsworth, *Lines on Tintern Abbey,* 1798).

We can gradually lose contact with that, become alienated even from ourselves, seduced into an excessively technological universe with plastic toys and cellphones. None of that is 'wrong' unless we lose a sense of proportion and see it as important. On a Cyprus holiday, Althea and I dined next to a young businessman accompanied by his lovely girlfriend. During the entire romantic and excellent meal on St Valentines Day, he talked incessantly over the phone to colleagues in several different countries about a land development deal.

Wilber (1979, preface) comments:

> *we create a persistent alienation from ourselves, from others, and from the world by fracturing our present experience into different parts, separated by boundaries. We artificially split our awareness into compartments such as subject vs. object, life vs. death, inside vs. outside, reason vs. instinct – a divorce settlement that sets experience cutting into experience and life fighting with life. The result of such violence, although known by many other names, is simply unhappiness. Life becomes suffering, full of battles.*

This is a struggle with perceived splits, looking through a glass very darkly.

The desire to control is the opposite of a genuine spiritual pathway. Any perception of the world as a series of technical difficulties risks losing the real sense of wonder and marvelling that Wordsworth communicates so well. We are already deep into this sort of society, relying on various forms of social engineering – failing to understand the essentially organic and intimately connected nature of our world.

Everything we do can become calculated, no longer trusting our true nature. It is necessary to reflect before we even walk or crawl.

> *Colour may blind the eyes.*
> *Sound may deafen the ears.*
> *Taste may dull the palate.*
> *Desire may trouble the heart.*
> *Excitement may confuse the mind.*
> *The Wise don't put their trust in how things seem.*
> *They follow gut feelings.*
> *This is their choice.*

(Freke, 1995, p. 46)

Merton (1965, p.23) comments on the essential dangers of the excesses of introspection:

> *The more 'the good' is objectively analyzed, the more it is treated as something to be attained by special virtuous techniques, the less real it becomes. As it becomes less real, it recedes further into the distance of abstraction, futility and unattainability. The more, therefore, one concentrates on the means to be used to attain it. And as the end becomes more remote and more difficult, the means become more elaborate and complex, until finally, the mere study of the means becomes so demanding that all one's effort must be concentrated on this, and the end is forgotten.*

I increasingly noticed that our university postgraduate students did work that was more and more distant from the frontlines in nursing and social work. Ten years ago they researched issues that had some direct relevance to services; nowadays they produce acres of literature courtesy of the internet and tons of stuff about research methods, but precious little that might improve the services next week or even next year. Reflection can become obsessive.

A few years ago a senior probation officer rang me. 'You don't know me but I want some advice. My secretary has been off sick for two weeks with probable leukaemia. I am fond of her and wish to know how she is. But if I ring up it will look as if I am trying to find out when she is going to return. I have no wish to pressurise her. But if I don't ring, she'll feel I don't care . . .' I responded very directly: 'Are you really fond of her?' 'Yes' he replied. 'Then immediately I put the phone down – ring her.'

In mental health, we have already built a high brick wall to protect against a necessary madness – a chaotic and potentially creative disorder. Occidental ideologies are kept distant from Western ideas and practice. Japanese approaches to personal growth, such as Morita and Naikan therapy, remain virtually unknown, in contrast to the great import of the martial arts such as judo and karate. (Reynolds, 1980). These particular therapeutic systems pose difficulties for the West because they are based on 'being' rather than on 'having', on quietness and even silence rather than talking.

'Mental illness' has become a sickness to be managed and sometimes 'cured'. In great contrast, Jamison sees her own manic depression in more complex ways, comprising both yin and yang.

> *The ominous, dark, and deathful quality I felt as a young child watching the high clear skies fill with smoke and flames, **is** always*

there, somehow laced into the beauty and vitality of life. That darkness
is an integral part of who I am, and it takes no effort of imagination on
my part to remember the months of relentless blackness and exhaus-
tion, or the terrible efforts it took in order to teach, read, write, see
patients, and keep relationships alive. (Jamison, 1995b, p. 210).

Transcendent experiences are more usually psychiatrised nowadays. Seeing
visions and hearing voices are categorised as psychotic in *DSM IV*.
Hallucinations result in yet more pills. Socrates commented rather more
wisely out of his own experience of hearing demons' voices: 'our greatest
blessings come to us by way of madness, provided the madness is given us by
divine gift' (quoted in Walsh, 1990, p. 90).

Thankfully, we have the beginnings of a more gracious and delicate psychiatric
understanding. Whilst mainstream psychiatry still favours drugs to treat
'voices' some dissidents see that as dangerous. Taylor, a Bradford psychiatrist,
comments: 'I don't think voices are necessarily signs of mental illness. For
some people, the experience is brought about by intense distress, and that tends
to get them into contact with mental health services.' (Moore, 2000, p. 46). We
have a slow move towards some levels of healthy diversity and humility.

Shamans
The shamans have an extremely long tradition. They were the healers in the
ancient tribes, still relevant in some parts of the so-called undeveloped world.
He or she is in touch with both the extreme pain and the joys of living,
described by Jamison above. This sort of journey is fraught with dangers and
through it the wounded healer develops a particular relationship with the
essential nature of sorrow and suffering. Through his or her gifts, knowledge
of alternative ways of living, the overall possibilities of the whole
community for survival can be increased.

Kalweit (1992, p. 248) looks at the basis of shamanic healing:

So what is healing, where does it begin, where does it end? Are we
really only trying to get rid of physical ailments and to balance psycho-
logical deficiencies? Or are we looking for more? Is it really the case
that all that needs to be healed is what is labeled illness in the hospital
and the psychiatrist's office? Certainly the first stage of healing is the
healing of body and mind. But the second stage is healing the 'ego
condition.' Here we open ourselves to a transpersonal, transtherapeu-
tic condition. On this level, healing is an expansion of perception and of
communication.

Many years ago I interviewed a social work student who wanted a placement with MIND. She was struggling with her social work course and life as a single parent. Her marriage had just ended in divorce. Towards the end of our encounter she broke down in tears. She sobbed: 'I suppose you won't taken me now, I've broken down.' I responded, recalling my own experience at Sussex, 'We will take you because you are crying.' It was sad that she was learning to think that strength meant becoming like a rock rather than a reed. Her suffering could become the start of an important journey.

There was a Zen master who returned home after a long journey to find the funeral taking place of a favourite daughter of friends and neighbours. A man found him in a corner weeping. 'How can you help your friends in their hour of need, if you're overwhelmed by tears?' The master responded: 'On the contrary, I can help best through my tears.' Of course he could. His contribution was to feel the full sorrow and tragedy of the event rather than to sit meditating in some corner.

The Zen teacher, Bernard Glassman (1998, p.34) writes of religious retreats in Auschwitz, the former concentration camp:

> *There are many ways to express a broken heart: tears, laughter, silence, dance, and even German lullabies. You don't find wholeness till you're ready to be broken. Evening after evening we found new ways to express our brokenness. Each time we did this, a healing arose. And in the mornings we always went back to Birkenau. It was an endless continuous practice.*

Ordinarily our wounds are hidden, protected from others. In this dreadful place it was impossible. Faced with this horror, people's wounds were opened wide and healing began.

The Norwegian painter Munch wrote of the ways in which creativity exists alongside profound anxieties:

> *My whole life has been spent walking by the side of a bottomless chasm, jumping from stone to stone. Sometimes I try to leave my narrow path and join the swirling mainstream of life, but I always find myself drawn inexorably back towards the chasm's edge, and there I shall walk until the day I finally fall into the abyss. For as long as I can remember I have suffered from a deep feeling of anxiety which I have tried to express in my art. Without anxiety and illness I should have been like a ship without a rudder.* (Hobson, 1985, P. 275)

The artist lives with an acute sense of impermanence; his painting, writing, music – constantly reflecting an acute sense of the ephemeral – the light is fading, the sounds dying away. Munch lived on the edge of a despairing chasm, threatening to pull him in – never to return.

Grof linked some transpersonal crises with these shamanic traditions.

> *In the experiences of individuals whose transpersonal crises have strong shamanic features, there is a great emphasis on physical suffering and encounter with death followed by rebirth and elements of ascent or magical flight. They also typically sense a special connection with the elements of nature and experience communication with animals or animal spirits. It is also not unusual to feel an upsurge of extraordinary powers and impulses to heal* (Grof and Grof, 1986, p. 7–20).

Traditionally the roles of client and professional existed in one person. Injury and vulnerability might also be deliberate. 'Genuine healers can injure themselves without a second thought; if they are holy, then their wounds heal by themselves. In this way they test their capabilities and provide proof of their healing ability.' (Kalweit, 1992, p. 36) This seems a bit ostentatious to me and a very long way from practical Zen.

My own practice is based on my personal experience of being battered as a child and running away to homelessness in London. This forged a strong desire to work with the socially excluded and marginalised. Social work has been a quest for meaning through clumsy attempts to serve others. 'Our suffering is a sacrifice, but often what we suffer from can be a gift of strength, like the shaman's wound becomes the source of his or her compassion.' (Halifax, 1994, p. 15).

This is the core of Glassman's broken heart – a form of awakening:

> *At some stage the hero's conventional slumber is challenged by a crisis of life-shattering proportions, an existential confrontation that calls all previously held beliefs into question. It may be personal sickness, as with the shaman; it may be confrontation with sickness in others, as with the Buddha. It may be a sudden confrontation with death.* (Walsh, 1990, p. 28)

My long experience of violence sometimes enables more direct communication with those who are battered, and especially the homeless. The initial 'mental' breakdown occurred at the London School of Economics. (Brandon, 1997.) I was exhausted, travelling three hours every day on the train to attend a professional social work course. Nanna was dying and my mother-in-law, with whom we lived, was also terminally ill. We were struggling with many marital problems; raising two young children; reaping a whirlwind of years of violence from brutal Dad; brain enzymes not processing properly; perhaps genetics because Dad was also a psychiatric patient. I rule out none but add another – a spiritual crisis.

What does that really mean? My ordinary ways of living in the world, frameworks of meaning, weren't working. I was pitchforked into despair. During this crisis I felt completely separated from the universe and other human beings; precariously perched on the edge of the unknown world. I felt overwhelmed, alone and misunderstood, mixed in with strong suicidal feelings. My everyday life was totally wrecked. Everything was worthless, disintegrated into dust. It had been a substantial illusion but nothing more.

There was nothing to hold on to, everything shifting in all directions. Those dark uncertainties were filled with great anxiety and gloom. I lived on the edge of nothingness for several months at a time, sometimes even years. Monthly I travelled by train to visit my Zen teacher and described living on the edge of oblivion. She congratulated me vigorously. 'Wonderful – David. It's going really well.' Whatever was going really well wasn't me.

I couldn't concentrate on what was happening around me. My scattered energy was fixed on so many negative things from the past and anxiety about the future. I wasn't engaged with others usually close to me – my wife and sons. They seemed distant – 'rather stranger than the rest.' (Clare, 1996) I couldn't feel their love. I was frozen, nobody could possibly understand what I was going through.

At infrequent times I emerged into the bright light once more. I blinked to see the immense wonders all around and the shadows melted away. Sometimes, coming from the shadows, I felt light and joyful, like brightly coloured balloons floating upwards. The suffering self was lost for a few hours or days and the way clearly marked, and then the darkness returned.

I am still engaged in that daily struggle that brings so much beauty and sorrow. The novelist Henry James described it well:

> *Life is, in fact, a battle. Evil is insolent and strong; beauty enchanting and rare; goodness very apt to be weak; folly very apt to be defiant; wickedness to carry the day; imbeciles to be in great places, people of sense in small, and mankind generally unhappy. But in the world as it stands is no illusion, no phantasm, no evil dream of a night; we wake up to it again for ever and ever; we can neither forget it nor deny it nor dispense with it.'* (James, quoted in Alvarez, 1974, p. 308)

Most days and weeks still feel much that way.

Shamanic training

Shamanism involves exploration of personal vulnerability, a continuous contact with the damaged side – wounds stemming from isolation, lack of love and developing ways of using these to reach out lovingly to others. Professional training usually strives to conceal such wounds. Social work books mostly discourage self-revelation whilst, in contrast, Shamans use 'wounds' overtly as a primary source of healing. This vulnerability involves 'the dissolution of the boundary between self and the world' (Kalweit, 1992, p. 71).

Shamanism returns to being human rather than acquiring masses of techniques that offer radical improvements. Shamanic practice turns its back on Homer's Calypso and the struggle to be superman or woman. Instead it undertakes a paradoxical journey, arriving back at the same place. On the day of my ordination I asked my abbot 'What does it mean to be a monk?' He answered 'Tomorrow morning, a Zen monk will wake up in your bed and go and get some breakfast.' I could have killed him and it took me years to appreciate his response.

The shaman's art is based on the nature of interconnectedness.

> *In old Earth cultures, the shaman is the servant of the people, the gods and ancestors, the creatures, plants, and elements. When the world is out of balance, the shaman redresses this disequilibrium. In these cultures, illness is understood as a loss of the sense of connectedness, of relatedness, of continuity – the experience of a kind of existential alienation.* (Halifax, 1994, p. 193)

This sort of approach calls for a different posture – knowing nothing.

> *How might an empty mind be used in psychiatric nursing practice? I can only speak from my own experience. For some time I have been part of a family team offering to meet with people characterized as having severe and enduring mental health problems who are also usually veterans of psychiatric services. Rather than 'therapying', we try to offer speculative comments to the people, which they may, or may not, find interesting. Early in my new experience, I found myself striving to divest myself of the belief that the theories that had been part of my professional socialization were more real, helpful, truthful than other, more vicariously adopted ideas. By doing so, I found that I could be more creative, playful, and interesting for the people who were listening.* (Stevenson, 1996).

A Shamanic training would involve these elements:

- *Wounds:* the shaman explores and uncovers his or her various wounds and stigma. For me, it was a long experience of violence, humiliation and anger. How can we use these experiences so that suffering can be forged on an anvil for healing? Newly forged it becomes the core of the healing.

- *Empathy:* the connections between us, the ability to put oneself in the shoes of the distressed other. Bertrand Russell meets the novelist Joseph Conrad:

At our very first meeting, we talked with continually increasing intimacy. We seemed to sink through layer after layer of what was superficial, till gradually both reached the central fire. It was an experience unlike any other that I have known. We looked into each other's eyes, half appalled and half intoxicated to find ourselves together in such a region. The emotion was as intense as passionate love, and at the same time all embracing. I came away bewildered, and hardly able to find my way among ordinary affairs. (quoted in Hobson, 1985, p. 276)

- *Loving-kindness:* to be a vehicle of affection for the world and the people in it; to make manifest the linking of all things. Schweitzer commented: 'the only ones among you who will be truly happy are those who have sought and found how to serve.' (quoted in Walsh,1990, p. 211).

> *Can I see another's woe*
> *And not be in sorrow too?*
> *Can I see another's grief,*
> *And not seek for kind relief?*

(Blake, 1794)

- *Rituals:* the silence and preparation in the car before entering the house or centre to start interviewing. It involves an obligatory conversation about the perfidious English weather; drinking any tea on offer. Leaving the various bureaucratic forms for the end so that they can be completed together, a practical act of unity; summarising what has been agreed and saying goodbye. These rituals are important for healing as well as for mind focusing. These rituals are jointly accomplished. It is vital for the client to be centrally involved.

- *Mindfulness*: quietening the mind; daily discipline turning interviews into a meditative experience; concentrate on keeping in the
  now; keeping the mind single pointed. This sort of learning means
  giving up what we thought we knew already. It means disposing of
  our excess baggage.

- *Mutual transformation*: this process of disciplined helping trans
  forms both sides, becoming one. We are not helping so much as
  both being helped. Both shaman and client are students learning to
  uncover the mysterious elements. 'All psychotherapeutic methods
  are elaborations and variations of age-old procedures of psycho
  logical healing.' (quoted in Walsh, 1990, p. 184)

One study shows that some mental health service users increasingly prefer
the perceived holism of complementary therapies to drug treatment. One user
comments: 'I have developed a style which combines a spiritual grounding
with a variety of therapies, such as the use of art, music, verse and knowledge
of stress management to help gain control over my emotions' (MHF, 1997).
Imagine what great healing could be brought by genuine collaboration
between nurses, doctors, social workers and other professionals, combined
with the experience and vision of users.

Traditional scientific methodologies have dangers but so do the excesses of
subjectivity – expressed in the self-indulgence of popular New Age systems.
Nowadays we are asked to trust all manner of snake oils: reflexology,
camomile teas, aromatherapy, 57 different varieties of counselling, often
peppered with a strong dash of astrology and tarot cards. They symbolise a
worrying flight from reason as well as a genuine quest for nonexistent certainties. They seek answers to the problems of ordinary living that arise out of a
profound dissatisfaction with the aridity of much contemporary psychiatry and
other professional disciplines. But just because we don't fancy the shadows in
Plato's draughty cave, doesn't mean we have to rent rooms in Disneyworld.

At the basis of all our healing is increasing self-awareness and compassion to
others. This asks us to be gentle with ourselves and others and to surrender
our different images of perfection as deluded measures of the world, and to
see it with honesty and love. There is a modern story of the holy fool
Nasrudin going to a bank to cash a cheque. The bank teller asks for some
identification. Nasrudin reaches into his pocket and pulls out a small mirror.
Looking at it he says: 'Yep, that's me all right.' (Kornfield, 1993, p. 163).
Now that is genuine self-knowledge!

Not knowing

The direct opposite of not knowing is pretending or even deluding yourself that you have knowledge. An American professor was anxious to learn more of Zen on a visit to Tokyo. Through the consulate it was arranged for him to visit a Zen master. Very carefully the master made tea whilst the professor chattered on about his readings of Zen. He talked of the books he'd reviewed, the seminars he'd attended, the important people he'd met. He continued his discourse until the tea was made and the master poured it into the cup held by the professor. The tea overflowed from the cup into the saucer but still the professor talked on. It was only when the tea poured from the saucer and onto the floor that he stopped and exclaimed: 'My cup is full'. The Zen master said softly: 'So I see.'

Montaigne (1958, p.255) had in mind people like this particular professor: 'The learned generally trip over this stone. They are always parading their pedantry, and quoting their books right and left'.

But these drives have all sorts of origins. Some of us are driven by self-importance; others like this Japanese farmer, by a desire for increased material comfort and concern for the family. Many years ago a hard-pressed farmer in northern Japan sought help from an old Buddhist abbot who he respected a great deal. 'I desperately need money. My daughter must get married soon and requires a dowry. My son needs more land and a house of his own. I need to clear my debts, so my wife and I can rest easy in our old age. Do you know any sure way of making gold?'

'Oh' said the abbot, 'What a relief, I thought you were going to ask something difficult. That's simple. Follow my instructions carefully and you will make lots of gold, quite sufficient for all your needs. First get a large cauldron full of water and bring it to the boil on a roaring fire. Then put into the water two large smooth stones, preferably from the beach. Add a pinch of salt and pepper and ten leaves of these herbs. Simmer for precisely two hours and the stones will have turned into pure gold nuggets.'

The farmer was extremely pleased. He listened intently and rushed off to try out the recipe after profuse thanks and many bows. The abbot shouted after him: 'Just one last thing. During the whole process you must not think of a green crocodile or else the whole process will fail.' 'I understand' he called back breathlessly.

Next week the abbot observed a head-bowed and defeated man. 'What happened?' he asked. 'Well', he explained, 'I got everything perfect – the cauldron, the boiling water, the pebbles, the salt and pepper and the herbs and the whole mixture is bubbling nicely when the image of a green crocodile enters my mind. The pebbles simple remain pebbles. The harder I try, the more the green crocodiles come into my head. I can't eat or sleep. I wish I was dead.'

As usual and most annoyingly, the Zen story ends just as it gets interesting. Perhaps the farmer eventually realises that the abbot had given him something much more precious. He had skilfully cut at the scales over the gold-seeker's eyes. Perhaps the farmer now understands that he's a shaman. Hopefully the 'failure' of the gold experiments is the beginning of liberation. What does it mean to have real wealth? How can we live with not knowing?

The Nobel laureate Richard Feynman commented on the same sort of approach.

> *You see, one thing is, I can live with doubt and uncertainty and not knowing. I think it's much more interesting to live not knowing than to have answers which might be wrong. I have approximate answers and possible beliefs and different degrees of certainty about different things, but I'm not absolutely sure of anything and there are things I don't know anything about, such as whether it means anything to ask why we're here... I don't have to know the answer. I don't feel frightened by not knowing things, by being lost in a mysterious universe without any purpose, which is the way it really is as far as I can tell. It doesn't frighten me.* (Feynman, quoted in Gleick, 1992, p. 438).

Now that is a million light years away from ignorance and close to humility. But as ever, the old *Tao Te Ching* was there a long time before Feynman.

> *It is healthy to know you know nothing.*
> *Pretending to know is a kind of sickness.*
> *Realising you are ill,*
> *Is the beginning of healing.*
> *The Wise are sick of sickness,*
> *And so they are well.*

(Freke, 1995, p. 116)

Chapter 5
Yin of Flowing

Highest good is like water. Because water excels in benefiting the myriad creatures without contending with them and settles where none would like to be, it comes close to the way. (Lau, 1963, p. 64)

'Going with the flow' was an old 1960s expression, somewhat infuriating and trendy with a hippie infusion. It was a great cliché, along with 'going to San Francisco with flowers in your hair', voluminous caftans and soft drugs. Did it mean anything? What was the flow and where did it come from? I am still struggling nightly with large doses of Quaker puritanism but pulled strongly towards intuition and 'hanging loose'.

In a way, the very moment we ask, any answer is already lost. We have climbed out of the swimming pool onto dry land. These sorts of queries can't part the water or come close to the Way – whatever that might mean. The way to be experienced in the whole. But I'm surrounded by a world in which everything is dissected and separated and little is ever seen in the round. There is, as usual, an old Hindu story. A little fish was swimming round and round. A large fish asked why. 'Because I am looking for the ocean.' 'You're in it. It's all around you', said the large fish. So the small fish was swimming around in the very solution it sought.

> *Those who flow with life well know*
> *They need no other force;*
> *They feel no wear, they heed no tear,*
> *Require no mending or repair.*
> (Lao Tzu, quoted in Adams, 1999)

But it's never as easy as that. Montaigne also had serious difficulties with flowing and pliability.

Life is an unequal, irregular, and multiform movement. Incessantly to follow one's own track, to be so close a prisoner to one's own inclinations that one cannot stray from them, or give them a twist, is to be no friend to oneself, still less to be one's master; it is be one's own slave. (Montaigne, 1958, p. 251).

I'm a great fan of Michel de Montaigne but I don't think he knew much about flowing.

Constipation

Our world is full of handbooks and videos. 'Do it yourself.' Distant learning is the latest fashion. Some of us work in universities and colleges constipated by modular systems, with an obsession for goals and learning outcomes. We want to be clever rather than wise.

> *But there is the irresistible temptation in us to find out how, which is to learn the secret by a linear, step-by-step method, or to be told in words. How is it that people ask for, say, dancing to be explained to them, instead of just watching and following? Why is there formal instruction to teach something so natural as swimming?* (Watts, 1979, p. 112).

The short answer is that we are all behaviourists now. We don't learn much any more by watching a real person practising a desired skill or by discovering the flow of his or her actions. But the flow is still vital.

Our human energy is extremely restless. We ceaselessly struggle to change the planet, to move this heap of soil over here and that rock over there. We are always moving from 'here and now' to 'there and then'.

> *In our everyday life we are usually trying to do something, trying to change something into something else, or trying to attain something. Just this trying is already in itself an expression of our true nature. The meaning lies in the effort itself. We should find out the meaning of our effort before we attain something.* (Suzuki, 1973, p. 122).

I'm easily seduced by the appearance of things; failing to look at the meaning of the effort.

Where are we all intending to go and by what means? Remember that splendid Spike Milligan story? He goes up to the railway ticket office and asks the pompous clerk: 'Can I have a return ticket please?' The clerk responds crossly: 'Where do you want to go?' Spike says beautifully: 'To here – you fool.' Of course he's correct – we're always returning to the place from which we started.

My life is full of constipated stupidities. Like Montaigne, I spend a great deal of time struggling hard against the grain of the wood, rather than working with it like any good carpenter. I'm imbued with a good deal of passion – mainly from self-righteous anger about the way things are and, especially, visions of how they ought to be (in my opinion). I spend a great deal of time fighting against the current flow. Inside me are powerful, sometimes overwhelming forces – seemingly from formative experiences. If my life flashed before me,

I would see my Dad in the mental hospital; his insane rage and my Mam bloody and beaten up by the coal fire, hair half pulled out; being wet and homeless on the London streets; vulnerable people abused in care homes; watching Sunderland football team win anywhere. . . Those snapshots involve enormous passion, feelings of complete injustice and total vulnerability that have indelibly marked the way I've lived.

So these internal forces drive me to swim strongly against 'natural' tides. I've found myself a completely isolated protestor against perceived injustice on so many occasions. It's close to karma. My style of combat has the major side effect of excluding most others. Working alongside Larry Gostin helped me to see that. For many years he was the legal director of MIND, the mental health organisation, and was an exceptionally gifted advocate and colleague.

We (or rather he) became involved in an important legal case. Patients from Calderstones (a mental handicap hospital) were protesting about their exclusion from the electoral roll and having no right to vote. Larry and I went together by car to Clitheroe to attend the hearing. There were about ten of us in the hall – some patients with staff, Larry and me. I sat beside Larry for support. I went to talk to a hospital staff member and then found that my chair had been pushed back so that Larry was now on his own. He needed to face the dragon, just like Beowulf, on his own – even if it meant damage and death. I looked in the mirror and saw we had the same fundamental nature.

> *Wise sire, do not grieve. It is always better*
> *to avenge dear ones than to indulge in mourning.*
> *For every one of us, living in this world*
> *Means waiting for our end. Let whoever can*
> *Win glory before death. When a warrior is gone,*
> *That will be his best and only bulwark.*

(Heaney, 1999, p. 46)

For Beowulf, this fighting against evil meant going with the flow, becoming part of the waterfall. It suited those days of dragons and sinister creatures, heroes and warriors. It was a period for action not reflection. For Larry and me the times were very different. We were supposed to reflect studiously, to negotiate, to mediate, to learn forgiveness – rather than to train as samurai in the pursuit of dark and threatening shapes. We live amid mountains of words and rules, not of swords and axes. We are supposed to be reasonable. Asking human beings to be reasonable is among the most unreasonable of requests.

Is this apparent difference in cultures – between the end of the first and the beginning of the third millennium – really genuine? Or is it that Satan simply got cleverer and retrained as an advertising executive? That reminds me of Milton's creepy description of Belial.

> *Belial, in act more graceful and humane;*
> *a fairer person, lost not Heav'n; he seemed*
> *For dignity compos'd and high exploit;*
> *But all was false and hollow; though his tongue*
> *Dropt manna, and could make the worse appear*
> *The better reason.*
>
> (Milton, Paradise Lost, Book II, 1, 44)

Effective packaging becomes everything. The gloss is more important than the content. The eminently presentable fallen archangel – Belial – was obviously 'on message'. It doesn't matter what he did but how it's all presented.

Busy

> *Rushing around like a demented bumble bee*
> *from meeting to meeting,*
> *person to person –*
> *feeding those fragmented illusions of importance*
> *when no-one will recall who we are*
> *less than five years after our death,*
> *exhausted but proud in our busyness*
> *with no longer any time to notice*
> *the snowdrops and the daffodils,*
> *the laughter of a small child*
> *the spring coming*
> *with a cascade of birdsong,*
> *its usual ordinary miracle –*
> *because there aren't enough hours in the day,*
> *although the nights are hollow with loneliness*
> *echoing the greed we call busyness.*

A social work friend told me the other day that she'd lost all desire to rescue people. It's been a profound drive within me, working with distressed clients, perhaps activated by the first memories of my parents continually quarrelling. Amongst my earliest memories is that of waking up in the dark, hearing them going at one another, voices raised, usually resulting in violence and then in feeling very fearful. I've been dealing with the rippling echoes of that terrifying chaos by helping others – counselling via the back door. The busyness that still stays with me is a reflection of that early desire to be doing things. My Dad hated me not doing something. Mam was always very busy – her skeletal hands blurring over the sewing or knitting; the immense roar of the industrial sewing machine as she made loose covers. It seemed a cardinal sin not to be making something.

My wanderings and ceaseless activity were ways of being out of the house – always a dangerous place. I was escaping not just geographically but into many other worlds, other levels of consciousness, what Mam scathingly used to call daydreaming. Books were the main portals for those vital journeys. They were an active dreaming, travelling to different places and in different spaces.

Dharma

I am walking slowly to work along the lovely River Cam, close to my Cambridge flat – shared with my wife. It's a relaxing walk I've done most mornings and evenings for nearly eight years. I work as a social work teacher at a university that often feels like a morgue. Whilst slowly walking, I wonder about the Dharma because Zen Buddhist monks are supposed to contemplate on such issues. My travelling mind keeps wandering and wondering.

After a few minutes I reach the gentle bend in the river where the kingfishers nest in the bank amongst the roots of weeping willows. It's more like a tiny cave than a nest. They are a great joy, waiting motionless on a branch and then suddenly darting in to the clear water to catch small fish. Its early spring and soon they'll breed and dart in and out to feed their hungry young chicks.

> *Bare willow strands*
> *flick the slow moving Cam*
> *and in the razored breeze*
> *darts the halcyon*
> *neon blue with flash of red*
> *low over muddied waters,*
> *seeking no great mysteries*
> *but fish.*

I wait patiently for them to do various tricks, such as skimming low over the water and meditating on the low branches, but not this particular morning. Perhaps they are having a lie in. Striving to see beyond the trailing willows I forget the Dharma and simply stand. For a few moments there is a merging of the mind with the slight breeze that moves the willow branches and intense watching. A story of the sixth Zen patriarch, Hui Neng, drifts into mind. Two monks were arguing fiercely. The first stated: 'The flag is moving.' 'No – it isn't,' said the second, 'the wind is moving'. Hui Neng overhearing, simply commented: 'The mind is moving.'

In a short time my keen expectations turn slowly to disappointment and I walk on kingfisherless. There are plenty of mallards, moorhens and a solitary swan, but no kingfishers. This is all very disappointing. Presumably they have some other business away from home, other fish to fry. A great pity for me because seeing them is like drinking a strong black coffee.

My mind returns to a patchy consideration of monkish issues, amid a hundred ordinary living worries also bubbling. What does it mean to be a Buddhist? What actually is Dharma? I start to define – following the Buddha as distinctively different from Christianity or Islam; precious Zen stories and pertinent quotes emerge. Could you recognise the Buddha from a rear view after all these centuries? Does this stupid Buddhist monk looking for the non-appearing kingfisher see something different, more or less profound, some marvellously illuminating framework? Of course not.

My left knee is sore from the early morning jogging. Do the left knees of Hindus or Jews ache in a different way? Does the kingfisher see anything different, declaring as it dives into the clear water, 'That's a middle-aged Zen Buddhist academic who believes I will come back as an eagle'? Or does it just catch the fish? And if there are differences, does it really matter? Is the orbit of distant Jupiter altered by even a quarter of a degree? Perhaps Chuang Tzu's butterfly turns into a kingfisher? My heart firmly says no to all these silly questions.

I'm wary of the whole spider's web of religious and political systems, something to do with being a Buddhist, whatever that is. You can get into embroidery so easily. They become gossamer prisons in a world of seductive mists and illusions; intricate ideologies, all sorts of isms. All isms suck – including Buddhism. They are well-wrapped packages of lucky charms to help deal with life's uncertainties – much of it cheap magic. I find it really difficult to sign up to anything. I am by nature an agnostic, a non-joiner that Zen fits.

I find believing so difficult. I partly envy and partly despise those who find faith easy. 'I believe.' They wear a necklace of creeds around their neck. I value doubting as a posture – a beginner's mind. I'm essentially suspicious of these long-winded Tibetan, Sanskrit, Pali, Japanese terms, esoteric languages that hide a load of oriental nonsense. I much prefer black pudding Zen to sushi after living in Preston for more than 17 years. I need a religious practice that deals with daily life in Cambridge. This uniquely academic city already has a huge surplus of ideas.

I'm struggling to live this ordinary life without worrying too much about whether anyone comes back as an eagle or a slug. I once asked my toddler son what the term reincarnation meant. He responded that it meant a tin of evaporated milk – Carnation Milk. An answer as good as any other. It took me away from wondering about stupid Buddhist ideas.

I'm putting one sore foot in front of the other as my mind goes all over the place – from kingfishers, to the morning's academic work, to a homeless project for which we are struggling to get funding . . . I'm inclined not to believe in reincarnation, and anyway it doesn't seem very relevant just walking along the slow-moving River Cam. I've terrible trouble dealing with the present life, never mind about what happened or might happen. So that makes me definitely not a card-carrying Buddhist, rather one of the Groucho Marx variety.

My life is a constant struggle between joy and despair, with ten thousand intermediate conditions. I am struggling to serve people, especially those who are vulnerable and excluded because that was my background as a child and homeless teenager. Usually I fail, whatever that might mean. I work hard but feel disappointed with myself. I lack the skills, the state of mind, have too much arrogance to serve in any real way. But I mostly get on with it on a daily and egotistical basis.

I laugh a lot. The study of self is not a serious endeavour. Dogen Zenjii said: 'To study the self is to forget the self.' Whatever I am is of no particular importance to kingfishers or anyone else. Do I exist? I mostly work with homeless people in this affluent city and try to teach social work students. Try is the operative word. I explore spirituality with the kingfishers as a serious ally. They are much more of what they are than I am. I stand and wait a lot beside the riverbank when they are about. They do what they want not what I desire. When I was ordained nearly 20 years ago my abbot, who had a terrific sense of humour, gave me a Japanese name – Kenshu, meaning one who seeks the core of spirituality. It should have been Japanese for 'one who can't see beyond the end of his nose!'

The teachers, the books on Buddhology, the various gurus and lamas are all way above my dizzy head. They live mostly in an exalted world with different levels of higher consciousness, high on the snowy spiritual mountains whilst I struggle daily through the stinking mud. Their grand views and paradoxical writings provide hope, mystery and occasional flashes of deep insight, but there is still dogshit all over my shoes. That's the trouble with looking up at the peaks whilst walking along the pavement by the river. Not that there are many mountains in flat East Anglia!

I am not troubled by the extreme high ground of Buddhism – the nature of karma, rebirth, the meaning of Dharma. I am troubled by ordinary events and decisions – lack of money, great excess of lust, struggling with fury, getting older, losing my hair, dying and death, sickness – concrete issues of impermanence, everything gradually passing away. I'm concerned about the people I love – my two sons, my wife; about friends and their troubles, about vulnerable clients struggling against sickness and poverty. I have barrowloads of difficult questions and but few satisfying answers. Well – they usually satisfy for a bit but have a limited shelf life, like perishables in the supermarket.

What the mountain of Buddhist books say, mostly doesn't help and sometimes actively hinders. No wonder my first Zen teacher banned me from reading for a whole year. I feel that other authors are so much further on. I go to Watkins bookshop in central London and gaze at all these glossy books. These authors have achieved so much, know so much, have their lives so well tailored. They live in eternal serenity whilst I'm often knotted and screaming inside like Jamison. I swing between social worker and lunatic so quickly.

I still get depressed, feel suicidal, get disparaged by their stories, concepts and definitions of graceful and grateful practice. They're spiritual smartarses, know-it-alls. They provide intricate ordnance survey maps of places high up in mountains that I'm never likely to climb, but hardly any maps of the stinking spiritual mud in which I daily struggle. I feel a great sense of frustration and envy when reading their books, so I read less and less nowadays. It's so easy to become a book junkie. Watts (1979, p. 119–20) commented acidly on those 'tourists who study the guidebooks and maps instead of wandering freely and looking at the view'. During a recent holiday in Paphos, Cyprus, I saw so many holidaymakers trying to cram that lovely world inside a camera.

This everyday journey through turmoil, love and hate is the essence of following the Buddha. Jesus also had insights about living life more abundantly, rather than arriving at some peak experience, attaining bliss or enlightenment, or any philosophical dissection of the meaning of Heaven. There are bliss as well as book junkies. I'm sure the Buddha was not a Buddhist, not that it matters so much.

Walking along the slow and muddy Cam, sometimes there are kingfishers and sometimes not. Sometimes ordinary life meets our flimsy expectations, but usually not. Sometimes we feel part of everything that is, and sometimes not at all. Sometimes we are filled with a strong feeling of love and unity, and sometimes we feel lonely, isolated and fragmented. This is the daily spiritual life, the immense pebble-polishing machine of the Dharma. We are rough pebbles, sometimes diamonds with direct experience of being polished. It's a tough experience. Everything that happens – despair, love, rage, disappointment – is the stuff of our training – the usually large gap between what we hope for or fear and what actually happens.

Boredom, as in monastic training, is the main key. We're stuck in this feeling that our life should be a sort of all-singing, all-dancing cabaret. We should be entertained and stimulated most of the time. Life is supposed to meaningful, with plenty of kaleidoscopic patterns. Boredom takes place when that is not happening. Our expectations are dashed.

God forgive me (though I don't believe in you), but I once told a young woman she was the most boring person I'd ever met. I had sat in a room in the health centre in Shoreham-by-Sea, West Sussex, pretending to be a mental health social worker, many years ago. She came in every Tuesday afternoon, depressed and boring.

This particular afternoon I decided to ambush her. She sat down and began a long monologue about how awful her life was: her husband didn't appreciate her; her children misbehaved; she didn't have any money. . . . After five minutes I cried out 'Stop.' She went silent and then asked: 'What's the matter?' I told her that she was the most boring person I'd met. There was a long silence and than we talked about what she was doing with both me and her husband and children. Luckily it worked. She reflected on her life and methods of communication. Her life improved.

But then I'm drifting back into a teaching and preaching mode. What do I know about anything? It's so easy to pretend you know something. It's the stock in trade of all academics, especially in the city of Cambridge. Leave it to the kingfishers.

On the very edge
of one sort of reality
at certain places and times,
robust boundaries become skin thin
as when an electric blue bird
flies low over ponds and streams
seeking fish
and catching me.

Selling water

'Selling water by the river' is an old and typically infuriating Zen paradox. It feels like you've been given something, then it's torn from your hands because it's on the end of strong elastic. In this vast river is an immense quantity of cool and pure drinking water, but most of the people living on the banks are dying of thirst. They don't know where to find the water, or if they do, how to get it out. A few people have learned this trick and keep all knowledge to themselves, becoming aqua gurus. They possess large buckets and make a very comfortable living selling full cups of the deliciously transparent elixir to the woefully ignorant at high prices.

It's against the vested interests of these families of water vendors to spread the information about water. It would ruin their whole business. They fill their buckets silently and secretly during the hours of darkness. How would they sell even a single drop of H_2O if everyone knew the secrets of the infinite river, had their own buckets and got it all for free? How would their children and grandchildren and other future generations ever make a good living? By being partial to themselves and their families – a basic human instinct – they prevent the vital and ordinary spread of compassion, knowledge and sustenance for all sentient beings.

I know this partiality all too well. My fear clouds over the love. I'm fearful of strangers and strange situations. I fear being overwhelmed. I want to conceal the sources of any special knowledge or skills I've got. Others might not value them or me and then where would I be? Genuine affection is everywhere but I often feel lonely – cut off and remote from those around. My stomach tightens up. I can't possibly live up to all those imagined expectations. I feel that others are cold and hostile, unwilling to share love and respect. Completely naked and vulnerable, without any social adornments, I could not be either loved or respected.

There was this gestalt drycleaner. A middle-aged man brought in a suit to be cleaned. 'My only daughter's getting married on Saturday. She's lovely and marrying a good man. The wedding has been so expensive I can't afford a new suit. Can you make this suit look much better?' The manager was delighted to meet the challenge. 'Of course we'll turn it out as good as new. We'll give it the full treatment, re-texture it. Come back on Friday and you won't even recognise it.' The man is handed an orange ticket and passes the suit over the counter. On Friday he arrives at the shop and hands the ticket to the young woman. She returns from the back of the shop after a few minutes.

'I'm sorry but I can't find anything to match this ticket.' 'But I brought it in the other day. My daughter is getting married tomorrow. The manager promised to make it look like new.' Just then he sees the manager and they exchange pleasant words about the impending marriage. 'About my suit. This young woman can't find it.' The manager responds: 'Yes. That's true. I took a closer look at your suit and it was awful and worn out so we threw it out with the rubbish.' 'But you can't do that. You promised me that it would look as good as new for the wedding tomorrow. You gave me your clearest promise.' The manager responds 'You've got some very serious psychological problems. You're trying to lay some stuff on me. I'm not here to live up to your crazy expectations and you're not here to live up to mine. Go and get some help and leave me and my business well alone.'

Well most of us, including me, can't live in a world as bewildering and changeable as that. We need commonsensical expectations that things will be done, be delivered roughly as promised; that what is said corresponds roughly to what happens. We live by some notion of informal contract, basically predicated on the assumed self-love of the other. As the eighteenth-century economist Adam Smith noted: 'It is not from the benevolence of the butcher, the brewer, or the baker, that we expect our dinner, but from their regard to their own self-interest. We address ourselves, not to their humanity but to their self-love, and never talk to them of our necessities but of their advantages.'(quoted in Sen, 1987, p. 23) The bride's father had calculated that the mythical manager had sufficient self-interest to match the breaking of promises with the business going bust. His calculation was wrong because something else was going on. Perhaps the manager was a moonlighting Zen master; much more probably he didn't much care about the business.

Underneath my profound fear of sickness, of losing faculties, of those dearest and nearest to me meeting serious tribulations, of dealing with gestalt drycleaners, I know the planet is full of love and joy. I know there is some fundamental warmth but I don't feel it that often. The grass grows, the sun often shines even in cloudy England, birds sing, and East Anglia has big skies and vivid sunsets. Human beings are born with a natural easy-going affection, dancing with nature, reaching out to others. Man is a social animal – a quality needed for basic survival. So why is life such a hard struggle? Why is the flowing river so often frozen?

Observe the young infant, positively bouncing and bubbling with love and warmth, and yet within a few years much of that natural and positive energy will be turned off. Spontaneous openness is covered with the dust of fear and suspicion. The fountain of joy is replaced by pain and suffering. I've watched young boys playing handball against a wall in Dublin, young boys with the faces of little old men. On this planet we have the knowledge and means to produce enough food to feed all people but hundreds of millions suffer from malnutrition.

The water vendors know the secret that love and joy are everywhere. They are part of everything that is, and on the occasional good days I also know and feel that. Every rock, every flower and blade of grass shouts out that secret. 'Knock and it shall be opened unto you. Seek and you shall find.' Some people, finding those sources of pure love, want to keep it to themselves. They are driven by insecure longings to own and control what can't be owned, and a deep wish to feel superior and special. This is an aspect of the 'Icarus Syndrome' – attempting to fly close to the sun melts the waxen wings, followed by the fatal fall to earth. Death follows hubris.

A few genuine prophets want everyone to learn of the infinite sources of love. They see it as a gift of Nature – not to be bought and sold like a commodity. They are frustrated by the fixed belief that both love and water are bought for a high price. People learn that real love has a high price tag, earned and deserved. Such beliefs prevent us from drinking freely so we're always thirsty inside.

Most people can't be loved for themselves. They can only be loved indirectly through a process of deserving. Others believe that love is complex,to be traded like stocks and shares. A Dow Index of affection going up and down. They have no experience of unconditional love. Instead of simply breathing in, love comes through expensive oxygen cylinders. They have little experience of the ebb and flow of life and love.

Dominion?
In our attempt to dominate the world we try to make it a product. This is the opposite of flowing. We don't want just to live in and on the world, but to shape and reshape it according to our imagination and desires. We can easily become arch manipulators with little respect for the planet, causing horrendous problems from global warming to the depletion of the ozone layer. In our fantasies, the earth has become our personal playground.

We try to dominate this small planet and ultimately the vast galaxies beyond. The great joke is that we have so little control over ourselves. There is a Zen story of a man on a runaway horse. A passer-by shouts: 'Where are you going?' The rider responds somewhat breathlessly: 'I don't know. Ask the horse.' It's just like the man who fell off the high building. As he hurtled past each floor, he was heard to cry out: 'I'm alright so far.' OK but the real test, the impact with the pavement, is yet to come.

A large proportion of our population are cut adrift socially and economically. They live daily in pain and indignity. They reside in overcrowded rooms, in damp flats, on vandalised housing estates; they and their children are sick. (Donnison, 1991, ch. 2). Poverty often involves social invisibility. These people, many old and female, don't have the money to live reasonably, whilst painfully surrounded by the icons of affluence.

Amid the pervasive cult of individualism, with its single measure of material success, we are frighteningly to blame for ourselves. The world exists to be made use of, to explore and exploit. Now the world is ours to win or lose in an unsustainable way. We are separated from the major social, economic and psychological forces – even from the gene pool; seemingly from any luck or chance. Success means exercising control, working hard, assuming power and responsibility, manipulating and exploiting others, presenting an efficient and attractive social face. All this is simple and untrue.

Huge numbers of young people are excluded from the possibility of valued ways of living. Their bleak future lies as part of the underclass, a world of drugs and theft, violence and sickness and bleak environments. Large sections of the welfare state are dismantled by successive governments and even the whole principle of social insurance is under attack. In one of the wealthiest nations ever known, whatever is needed cannot or should not be afforded. We are dismantling these various financial supports because it causes those in chronic poverty to become socially and economically dependent, which of course is bad for them!

Debates on social and economic inequality seem irrelevant in a culture of personal responsibility for misfortune and even for sickness. As we saw earlier, sickness becomes a new form of immorality. The sick are culpable because they eat and drink far too much, have the 'wrong'kind of diet, smoke cigarettes, consume dangerous drugs, take far too little exercise, risk AIDS with unsafe sex. . . . . Assigning blame is no way to understand and treat illness and inequality.

Social and economic inequality is a huge issue.

*Take the debate over the NHS, we are apparently suffering from
tremendous shortages in hospital beds and nurses; it seems vital for
patients to have access to all sorts of high tech facilities? But why?
Why is an expansion in plastic surgery so crucial? Why do we spend
time debating the provision of surrogate parenting on the NHS? Why
do we value high tech surgery so highly? Why don't we take the health
needs of hundreds of thousands of children living in poverty more
seriously? Simple – because they have little power, no political clout*
(Collee, 1996, p. 62).

We naturally focus on the social and economic issues that are sexy and interesting. dot.com companies; e-coli virus. It's really difficult to get interested
in run-down inner city centres, illiterate kids, demoralised schools. It is
boring unless the kids are ours and they're going to those shabby schools. It's
much easier to condemn the guilty teachers and parents than to analyse the
complex social and economic issues that contribute to those problems.

The newspapers are currently full of photos of Romanian women, mostly
gypsies, with babies in their arms, begging in central London; Eastern
European youths trying to clean car windscreens at the traffic lights.
Apparently this involves 'aggressive begging'– a term that nobody seems able
to define but which everyone seems to know the meaning. The number of these
individuals is very small but reading the newspapers one would imagine that
the whole of our civilisation was under attack! Hardy (2000, p. 22) comments:
'Everyone in the land should be ashamed and embarrassed that the politicians
and media hacks who claim to speak for us are trying to turn these women
[Romanian gypsies] into hate figures.'

We are in danger of creating the horrific and demonic 'Other'figure. Zohar
and Marshall (1994, p. 168) comment:

*if our attitudes towards society's most deprived outsiders are mecha-
nistic attitudes, if we perceive them as wholly other, as objects of our
pity and fear, as a problem to be overcome or a threat to be defended
against, these attitudes may evoke the behaviour that we most fear, the
rage and violence that do indeed threaten us, our property and our
daily activities.*

Such fears are not primarily about them, but about us. We begin to think in
macho ways that zap social problems, rather than perceiving them as part of a
wonderfully complex web. Our preoccupation is with building egos.

*The ego is strengthened by the power-based way of thinking that leads
to an objective, controlling, domineering, masculine kind of knowledge.
An imaginative, intuitive, receptive kind of knowledge is grossly undervalued in today's social work thinking and the undervaluing of certain
client groups can be ascribed to this fact.* (Wilkes, 1981, p. 111)

The demonisation of groups in our society – gypsies, drug addicts, homeless
beggars – has a long tradition.

*I remember from my history of the Holocaust that the Nazis started
their killing with prisoners, and mental patients, and people with
mental retardation. . . . Once a society starts needing to see people as
less than human, as devoid of worth, as 'useless eaters' to use the Nazi
term, it is a habit that tends to grow.* (Schwartz, 1992, p. 199)

This constipated impatience can be immensely dangerous, but so is demonisation. I remember the intense and righteous passion of a man in Blackburn:
'Everyone who believes in capital punishment should be hanged'.

Brief encounters

I began attending regular therapy groups in the early 1970s. These were
amongst the first encounter groups; 15 nervous strangers sitting on large
cushions in a big circle doing breathing exercises, meditating and exploring
boundaries once a week. In the beginning my attendance was based on ratio-
nalisation about learning new techniques to help people in the local health
centre where I worked. I soon learned how much help I needed.

The groups began rather self-consciously but people relaxed as we discovered one another. It was marvellous, if rather un-English, to be hugged and
cuddled so often. The leader encouraged expression in actions as well as
words. We danced energetically to samba music, practised various forms of
meditation, worked on Tai Chi postures. Many feelings were deeply buried
and only emerged from great suffering. Watching other group members go
through intense pain from childhood was frightening and overwhelming. I
was still trying hard to 'understand', to work things out intellectually. At first
I sat on the outside of these groups like a spectator at a football match, but
during the long fourth session I crashed from theory to involvement. An
older woman resented my detached, judgmental glances and what she
viewed as a general feeling of superiority. It was spat out from between
clenched teeth. I was bewildered and then great rage rose in my throat.
Enormous energy waves flowed through my body.

At the leader's suggestion I went to the centre of the large human circle, carrying a big cushion and punched choking force through my fists on it. I could hardly breath and coughed throughout the frenetic pounding. My fists were tightly clenched and still more energy rose up. The cushion seemed too tiny for the rage. I was suffocating from this vast surplus. As if from a long way off, I heard him suggest lying flat on my back. Six male group members firmly held me down. Their combined weight was crushing. My hands and feet were pinned firmly to the floor and I struggled to get up. At one point I almost succeeded, half stood with people hanging on, but was thrust down again.

Suddenly the intense energy evaporated. For a few moments I felt hollow, followed by heaving sobs – painful expressions of chronic sorrow. Memories from childhood, apparently long forgotten, took fresh possession over my mind. I could hear my detached voice assume, without conscious will, the thin tones with the broad Durham dialect of my early childhood. It poured on and on without conscious control.

I relived rather than remembered a kaleidoscope of events; saw and smelled the raw poverty of my home town Sunderland. Saw people drinking dark tea out of bean cans; large blackened kettles on shining hearths; rusting pithead machinery and the huge shipyard cranes; saw my father leering aggressively, felt his index finger dig in my chest, heard him arguing interminably; wanted to sleep but his desperately angry voice went on and on – 'That's right, that is right, isn't it ?' and the sneer up against my face got closer. Such a mixture of fear and rage came in ocean waves over my wracked body.

Saw Dad beating up mother – whole hanks of hair pulled out and head bleeding; felt frightened and small – nothing in the world that I could do; made contact with overwhelming hate and resentment. Hated the vicious beatings round my head; felt his stone fist beat into my skull, my head exploding in pain again; recalled his all-embracing sarcasm, his snarling face. The strong stocky body leaned over me and poked its finger deep inside my mind. Poke, poke, poke until I had to withdraw to survive although I wanted to stand courageous. I wanted to kick out fiercely at his strong legs. I resented the paralysing self-pity. I couldn't balance on my uncertain legs.

Ten thousand scenes of rejection and violence passed through my mind. My whole spine vibrated with surging energy until I became clearer and calmer. At the end I was physically and mentally exhausted, but buoyed up with warm affection and hugs.

A busy week later, at the health centre, even the thought of the group made me feel sick. The hurried slices of buttered toast washed down by black coffee at breakfast threatened to escape. Since the last group I'd done my mental health work on automatic pilot. Now I invented ten thousand reasons for not going. I had too much work; too many urgent referrals; numerous after-care visits; too tired and depressed. I felt too sick to make the train journey to London. After lunch I decided to go.

From that decision a great change took place. A tide of warmth and comfort eased all physical unease. A mound of heavy rocks fell off my back. Without intention, I touched a source of inner strength, becoming a multicoloured bubble of lightness and pleasure. I chuckled quietly at the absurdity, lightly bubbling through ten thousand illusions. I enjoyed the three-hour group. People smiled at my sunshine, except it wasn't mine. ' My little ray of sunshine' Mam called me when I was a toddler, and sang her favourite song: 'You are my sunshine; my only sunshine, I'll always love you when skies are grey. . . .' Anything and anybody set off a pleasurable echoing laughter. I accepted myself. I could see the stupidity but it was gently amusing. I'd escaped the straitjacket and my attention was infinitely heightened. A stone statue outside in the garden inspired; the bricks of the house opposite became a painting; the sound of people walking was a wonderful symphony.

This peculiar experience lasted three days and slowly evaporated in the fresh coastal air and the routine of social work and family life. It was disconcerting for colleagues at work. They much preferred me chronically depressed. A few months later I gave up my local government job. I had a secure career, eminently suitable for a married man with two children, just qualified as a psychiatric social worker. At 30 years old I was very young for a mid-life crisis.

Until that time I had had an intense ambition to be the youngest Director of Social Services – super social worker with big S knickers and T shirt, jumping tall buildings. In charge of a large department, all sorts of visionary and radical changes would become possible. This ambition lost any meaning. After the groups it fell off like the skin of a snake. I wanted to return to homeless people, return to the roots to understand more about the ways in which people got rejected and socially excluded. Instead of rising ever upwards in the local government stratosphere, I went to work at Christian Action – a small, chaotic and struggling organisation based in London, working mainly with homeless women. The job had poor pay, horrendously long and antisocial hours, cosmological responsibilities and lacked career structure. Wonderful. I felt such a sense of freedom from the bureaucratic constipation of local government.

Flowing

Peter Brook (1972, p. 47) described conducting an orchestra:

> *we recognize that magical thing called music can come from men in white ties and tails, blowing, waving, thumping and scraping away. Despite the absurd means that produce it, through the concrete in music we recognize the abstract, we understand that ordinary men and their instruments are transformed by an art of possession. We may make a personality cult of the conductor, but we are aware that he is not really making he music, it is making him – if he is relaxed, open and attuned, then the invisible will take possession of him; through him, it will reach us.'*

The sum is greater than all the parts. What comes from the orchestra or the theatrical company is much more than the playing of the individual violinists, percussionists or actors. They have been 'possessed', taken over by the spirit, to make this illuminating sound. Their individual self-consciousness is overwhelmed by the harmony of the different parts of the orchestra. It flows right through them all.

When training social work students or counsellors in video laboratories, their efforts and self-consciousness greatly obstruct any result. Thrusting egos get in the way. Each student concentrates on what he or she is trying to do, instead of just getting lost in the whole process. The music of the practice interview is lost. They are captured on videotape earnestly looking at and listening to themselves. They are strutting the stage rather than letting vital energy flow through them.

> *Tis God gives skill,*
> *But not without men's hands; He could not make*
> *Antonio Stradivari's violins*
> *Without Antonio.*
> (Eliot, quoted in Brandon and Atherton, 1996, p. 20)

God, possession or both are necessary, as well as the immensely skilled hands and patience of Stradivari. Somehow the social work students must get out of the way, forget themselves – so the whole process can flow, free of obstacles. They have to forget everything they've ever read or learnt about interviewing to get into a state of 'beginner's mind'.

This spiritual core was described in 1660 by the Quaker James Naylor. He had been robbed and bound some miles north of Huntingdon and he died about two hours later:

> *There is a spirit which I feel that delights to do no evil, nor to revenge any wrong, but delights to endure all things, in hope to enjoy its own in the end. Its hope is to outlive all wrath and contention, and to weary out all exaltation and cruelty, or whatever is of a nature contrary to itself. It sees to the end of all temptations. As it bears no evil in itself, so it conceives none in thoughts to any other.* (Religious Society of Friends, 1960, section 25).

Ceaseless flowing is not easy. It's not about being nice. It is about being a seamless part of everything, one's true nature finding expression. Einstein wrote in a similar vein:

> *A human being is part of the whole, called by us the universe. A part limited in time and space. He experiences himself, his thoughts and feelings, as something separate from the rest, a kind of optical delusion of his consciousness. This delusion is a kind of prison for us, restricting us to our personal desires and to affection for a few persons nearest to us. Our task must be to free ourselves from this prison by widening our circle of compassion to embrace all living creatures.* (quoted in Suzuki, 1999, p. 36).

This involves shedding our continuing partiality to ourselves, usually called egotism. We experience the whole world coming in through our skin and our insides merging with the outsides. We release ourselves from the prison that never really existed.

It's hardly possible for the billions of small fishes swimming in the ocean to see and experience the flow, the whole of the fluid process. They can only experience a tiny fragment of it and imagine it's the whole. This gives them a spurious sense of separateness, of individual significance. The same is true of us. As a tiny part of a complex social and biological system, it is difficult to see what we accomplish. Most of the connections and networks are invisible to us. On one level we are no more significant or less significant than anyone else. But still I struggle vigorously to feel important, to find significance. Such stupidities are the stuff of everyday living.

Chapter 6
Yang of Discipline

The Way out of Suffering means to be prepared to sweat white beads,
for it entails bearing what is unbearable and enduring what is unen-
durable. (Zen Master Hakuin, quoted in Schloegl, 1977, p. 63)

That's quite enough of fluffy marshmallows of love and compassion. What
about hard-nosed Yang? Hakuin's words are really tough. What about discipline, unpopular in our easy-going, easy-living society – the very antithesis
of comfort. It involves going through much pain and suffering, going against
the grain. What's the modern equivalent of samurai training? Prospective
Zen monks sat in the deep snow outside the monastery gates for three days
and nights to test the firmness of their resolve. If they survived, they got a
welcome and presumably a blanket and some hot sushi. If they had any sense
at all, they ran away.

My first Zen teacher wrote:

I once asked the head monk whether it was necessary to be so frightfully
severe with the young postulants who were blue in the face from exhaus-
tion, fear and anticipation of further trials. I asked whether they had to
be man-handled and thrown out in this way on top of being frightened
and in pain from their crouching. The head monk nodded and
explained: 'Yes; but it serves a dual purpose. Seen from their side, it is
the hardness of the test, the fear of the unexpected that comes with it,
and the awe.   It is necessary for them; we always tell them, if you
really want to come in, you must leave your self outside, then you will
have no difficulty in the training. But if you take yourself inside, you will
have nothing but difficulties yourself, and make difficulties for the
community. (Schloegl, 1977, p.35)

Those words contain a good measure of common sense, mixed with a big
handful of sado-masochism. Real discipline contains no sado-masochism,
but is a serious attempt to melt our encompassing shells.

It is only by a construct of the Western mind that we believe ourselves
living in an 'inside' bounded by our own skin, with everyone and
everything else on the outside. The place where transitional
phenomena occur . . . might be understood in this new paradigm of the

> *self, to be the permeable membrane that suggests or delineates but*
> *does not divide us from the medium in which we exist.* (Barrows, 1995).

We are held in by these intensely suffocating frameworks. Spiritual practices are supposed to offer liberation. Wilber (1984) beats us over the skull on radical religion:

> *a way of creating meaning for the separate self; it offers myths and*
> *stories and narratives and rituals and revivals that, taken together,*
> *help the separate self make sense of, and endure the slings and arrows*
> *of outrageous fortune… religion has also served – in a usually very,*
> *very small minority – the function of radical transformation and liber-*
> *ation. This function . . . does not fortify the separate self but utterly*
> *shatters it.*

This breakthrough requires a particular form of discipline. It involves looking deep into ourselves, so that we can fully experience the inner and outer worlds coming together. That is a good deal more painful than sitting in the snow for three days and nights. 'The nature of Zen does not lie in scholarship, philosophy, in the Buddhist doctrine, and not even in zazen, in other words Zen. It lies in one thing alone, namely seeing into the Buddha nature that is in each person'. (Trevor, 1969, p. 95) This means living everyday life with acceptance and attention.

Monastic discipline
I vividly recall my first experience of a Zen monastery many years ago, entered without kneeling in the deep snow. It seemed a place of great awe and fear, of mystery and uncertainty. The building was always freezing cold and there was never enough to eat or drink – certainly insufficient for real creature comfort. We began our immensely long day – seemingly in the middle of the night – by chanting the deep sleep loudly and unmusically from our lungs and eyes, usually some time before four in the morning. We walked everywhere quietly and with dignity but were still frequently rebuked for making too much noise. The Shhhhsh from awesome teachers was the main sound of the day.

The days were long, silent and exceedingly disciplined. The chief spiritual weapon was boredom. There was nothing of any interest, nothing for the hungry ego to grasp – no TV or radio, newspapers or magazines, no entertainment of any sort. Our minds desperately desired something or anything. Thoughts scattered back to the family, work and leisure. We became hungry ghosts with hour upon hour stretching interminably onwards. We sat painfully cross-legged, the silence punctuated only by the sound of heavy breathing and the tinkling bell as the meditation leader began and ended each session. Our minds were in a complete turmoil, though our bodies held still as the monitor passed by with the awakening stick. Frequently we bowed to be hit with the stick on painful backs. The bell brought a brief relief, accompanied by complex rituals. Sometimes, after several hours of sitting, we could hardly walk out of the meditation hall.

Most of the day was spent in silent meditation, eating and drinking, followed by hard labour in the garden. At set times, we listened to a Dharma talk from teachers and chanted lustily once more, followed by blessed sleep. But for me sleep was not blessed. I sobbed for hours in a lumpy bed. My fears were immense and could not be kept at bay. The dawn came much too soon, with the birds singing and the prospect of yet another terrifying day. Then came intensely energetic services with more tinkling bells, much prostration followed by awesome chants – chanting the impossible vow: – 'to save all sentient beings'.

Nervously I once asked my Zen teacher: 'What's the point of all this long sitting and severe discipline over so many days? Why are we doing it?' She replied with a hint of a smile: 'Well – you know at the end, that nothing quite so awful will happen to you for a long time.' And as I learned, she was usually right.

Months later I wanted desperately to leave. I explained that I was not sufficiently intelligent or courageous to endure the severe course. 'It's not for me. I'm going crazy. It is too disciplined and needs an enormous capacity for the endurance of suffering. I'm being compelled to look at parts of my life that I need to avoid. I am going home to resume my family life and work.' She stood firmly in front of me and announced fiercely: 'David – you may sit or you may die, but you're not leaving.' I stayed, and in a short time, felt more at peace with the inflexible training rhythms.

Suzuki (1973, p. 27) said of discipline:

> *Doing something is expressing our own nature. We do not exist for the sake of something else. We exist for the sake of ourselves. This is the fundamental teaching expressed in the forms we observe. Just as for sitting, when we stand in the zendo we have some rules. But the purpose of these rules is not to make everyone the same, but to allow each of us to express his own self most freely.*

Archery

I must have bought more than a dozen copies of Herrigel's marvellous book 'Zen in the Art of Archery' (1985). Very wisely – friends borrow and never return it. Presumably they need its wisdom. It's about discipline, but of a kind quite strange to Western minds. It's not about marching or holding your belly tight. It is even less about shooting arrows accurately (though that does take place) and more about facing fears, especially of death, dying and living.

Herrigel describes archery training for battle:

> *What is very much more difficult and of truly decisive importance is the task of stopping the pupil from thinking and spying out how he can best come at his opponent. Actually he should clear his mind of the thought that he has to do with an opponent at all and that it is a matter of life and death. To begin with, the pupil understands these instructions – and he can hardly do otherwise – as meaning that it is insufficient for him to refrain from observing and thinking about the behaviour of his opponent. He takes this non-observation very seriously and controls himself at every step. But he fails to notice that, by concentrating his attention on himself, he inevitably sees himself as the combatant who has at all costs to avoid watching his opponent.*
> (Herrigel, 1985, pp. 99–100)

This is a spider's web covered in super glue. So now you know and understand – oriental bow and arrow in your hands and nothing at all in your head. But it's not so easy. Herrigel is full of observations about purposelessness. The discipline has no point, hopefully unlike the arrows. To get past the duality of living, going towards some sense of wholeness is the 'aim' not the target. The archer, bow, arrow and target all become one.

The social work or counselling student faces the distressed client. The professional's head is stuffed full of a patchwork of wisdom and nonsense; eyes focused on the bow and arrow, wide of the target. He or she has read all the introductory books, attended a series of interviewing lectures, listened to the training tapes, watched all the videos and now boldly faces the client. For the next half an hour or so, all of that porridge of theory and practice, anxieties and neurosis can only obstruct flowing communication. The discipline of just sitting in the chair and focusing the mind is everything.

But the reality of nervous inexperience lies in watching ourselves rather than in being centred, walking into lamp posts whilst musing on the nature of the world. Did we remember to switch off the gas back at home? Have we parked the car correctly? What do those single yellow lines on the road mean? Is the question we've just asked relevant and wise? Our minds are flitting all over the place, completely without discipline, so that little energy remains for communication. So we try even harder. Attention. The sweat trickles from our brows as we concentrate and the situation worsens. We are stuck in a losing battle to unite the different parts, which were never separated. Watching ourselves, watching ourselves. . . . 'What is she thinking about the questions I'm asking? What am I feeling about what she's probably thinking?'

Pirsig comments:

> *If you want to build a factory, or fix a motorcycle, or set a nation right without getting stuck, then classical, dualistic subject–object knowledge, although necessary, isn't enough. You have to feel something for the quality of the work. You have to have a sense of what's good. **That** is what carries you forward. This sense isn't just something you're born with, although you **are** born with it. It's also something you can develop. It's not just 'intuition', not just unexplainable 'skill' or 'talent'. It's the direct result of contact with basic **reality**, Quality which dualistic reason has in the past tended to conceal.'*
> (Pirsig, 1976, pp. 277–78)

He is commenting on the insufficiency of these sorts of posture, especially those that are dualistic.

> *Following the Way of Heaven is like being an archer.*
> *Aim not too high – not too low.*
> *Stress the string*
> *Not too little – not too much.*
>
> (Freke, 1995 p. 122)

Remember the three statisticians who practice archery as a hobby. The first archer aims at a squirrel on a tree trunk and the arrow thuds into tree, exactly one metre higher up than the squirrel. The second marksman aims and hits the tree exactly one metre lower. The third archer shouts: 'We've hit it.' Unfortunately neither trees nor squirrels are too impressed by the law of averages.

Man of Tao

Our methods of learning can be essentially obstructive. They dice the world into the ten thousand lifeless bits allegedly making up the whole. Watching TV chat shows (simply for sociological reasons) I am struck by how much the audience looks at the TV monitors, to observe themselves, rather than at the 'star'. For them the TV process itself and their own appearances constitute the stars, not the famous interviewers – Oprah Winfrey, Jerry Springer, Esther Rantzen. . . . We can easily lose the whole point of the process. It's difficult to show videos to students nowadays because everyone fancies themselves as film producers. They can easily end up criticising the lack of zoom or the excessive use of soft focus, and not seeing the recorded communication.

It is easier to get into a hole than to gain a whole. We must move beyond fashionable views of slicing things up into learning objectives, tasks and processes, detailed instructions for assignments. Our flesh should be touched by the reality rather than what we'd like to happen. Things and people rarely fit in with our ideas and beliefs, so we have continuously to strip down and even ditch precious ideologies. As Feynman commented during the investigation of the failure of the space shuttle 'Challenger': 'For a successful technology, reality must take precedence over public relations, for nature cannot be fooled.' (Gleick, 1992, p. 428). However complicated and smart the ideologies we have, nature will find large gaps between what we believe and what is 'real'. Whatever we've learned to believe about distressed people, won't hold much water out there in the swamp with the crocodiles.

In a similar vein but rather more dangerously, Gould wrote of periwinkles: 'Some beliefs may be subject to such instant, brutal, and unambiguous rejection. For example, no left-coiling periwinkle has ever been found among millions of snails examined. If I happen to find one . . . a century of well-nurtured negative evidence will collapse in an instant.' Shortly afterwards he received by post a photo of a left-coiling periwinkle, sent by the curator of mollusks at the British Museum. This 'nasty ugly little fact brought down a conceptual edifice' (Gould, 1994, pp. 451–55)

Nobel laureate Richard Feynman, was a real man of the Tao. He intensely despised knowledge based on 'words about words' and how

> much of it was part of the American education, a mind-set showing itself not just in the habits of students but in quiz shows, popular what-you-should-know books, and textbook designs. He wanted everyone to share his strenuous approach to knowledge – finding things out. He would sit idly at a café and cock his ear to listen to the sound sugar made as it struck the surface of his iced tea, something between a hiss and a hustle, and his temper would flare if someone merely asked for

an explanation. He respected only the not-knowing, first-principles
approach: try sugar in water, try sugar in warm tea, try tea already
saturated in sugar, try salt . . . see when the whoosh becomes a fizz.
Trial and error, discovery, free enquiry. (Gleick, 1992, p. 284)

He resented the hollowness of standardised knowledge. Rote and conditioned learning drained away all that he valued in science: the inventive soul,
the habit of seeking better ways to do anything. He believed that his
knowledge-by-doing 'gives a feeling of stability and reality about the world
and drives out many fears and superstitions' (ibid.).

He liked to strip the brambles of ideologies away from reality. He used real
sugar lumps and genuine tea as weapons to reveal what happens right in front
of our eyes, rather than adhering to pet theories. As my first Zen teacher said:
'You may sit or you may die but you're not leaving.' Feynman's 'Nature
cannot be fooled' statement arose from a profound respect from repeatedly
rubbing up against it and finding out over and over again that you were
mistaken. This was an irresistible way to learn humility.

Long ago in an ancient Japanese monastery there was an intense debate about
the taste of seawater. Some scholars said it tasted like this and others, just as
strongly, that it tasted like that. The debate continued for many years and
considerable heat was generated. One can imagine a carefully constructed
theology of marine water. A young monk decided to find out directly, in the
best Feynman tradition. The monastery was very far from the sea, but as
Japan is an island, with beautiful simplicity he walked in a reasonably
straight line and reached the seashore after many weeks. Joyfully he ran
down to the waves, cupped his hands in the water and tasted it. In that single
moment he knew the answer.

In stark and deeply depressing contrast, a close friend rang me. She was
doing an Open University (OU) course. She had been a schoolteacher
working with young children for years and was now studying again with joy.
Well – she had been until the day before. Her tutor had rung her. 'Hello – I
thought I'd give you a ring. We know you put a lot of effort into your assign-
ment, a lot of passion and industry. However you didn't pay full attention to
the designated texts, and used arguments and references not contained in the
guidance notes. I've not read some of the references. Well for those reasons
we are marking you down.'

That's an extremely long way from Feynman. My friend was pressured to learn by rote as a student, using the agreed rail tracks, following the syndicated instructions, sticking to the common references because not to do so was a minor offence that tutors could not possibly remedy through additional reading. There was no biting of the sovereign to test the quality of the gold in this dark OU world. Everything was processed through a dozen carefully selected filters.

God help any young Einsteins studying in the early twentieth century. Imagine he submits his ideas on the laws of relativity? His tutor responds: 'What's all this then? I asked for plain Newtonian material and get obscure rubbish about light bending. Do you think you're Yuri Geller or somebody? We've given you a D. You're lucky it wasn't an E. Next time give us good old Isaac, the Grantham Guru and we'll award a B or A. Stick with what everyone already knows, sternly resist this temptation to push back the frontiers of knowledge – for God's sake. Do you think you're Albert Einstein or something? How are you going to get a comfortable, well-paid merchant bank post if you're always on some abstruse intellectual exploration?'

Chomsky comments à la Feynman:

> Students in European universities are not given enough encouragement to challenge the assumptions of Professors. Continental Europe still retains a rather authoritarian structure in the university system, with deference/authority relations built into cultural patterns. . . .
> What we know intuitively seems to lie far beyond what we can understand intellectually. (Pacitti, 2000, pp. 14–15)

We desperately need Feynman and Chomsky's approach to the helping of others, a mixture of irreverence and respect for intuition. Our best intentions can be a form of therapeutic evangelism, a psychological steeplechase for unwary clients. So many times I've become enraged and deeply disappointed when someone in distress does not respond to my favourite techniques. I'm practising a wonderful technique and some stupid client is insufficiently sensitive to react positively. Inside my skull a voice screams out – 'Bring me a better client.' But the *Tao Te Ching* is right, as usual. 'When being of service or caring for others, don't overdo it, Meaning – let go your ideas about how it should be' (Freke, 1995, p. 103).

'Letting go' is not a phrase we usually associate with discipline. And yet it is the highest of skills, more painful than simply acquiring facts and figures and new concepts. It's like tearing elastoplast off chest or arms. It means shedding cosy ideas so that reality can get closer. This shedding always involves the risk that what we believe proves totally misguided. As a small child on a beach I watched a hermit crab changing shells in a rock pool. It shed its small shell for a larger one – a few moments of great danger needing considerable care and attention. For those moments it was soft and unprotected.

The archery lessons show the essentials. We don't need to concentrate on the target but on the bull. Not the bull in the target but the one (sometimes called the ox) deep inside. This savage and undisciplined beast wants to do things, its way and in its own time. It knows how others should live, how to solve personal problems. Helping becomes simply manipulating distressed others. Professionals who think they know how others should live are dangerous.

Bullish
The best known expression of the Zen pathway (more accurately called *ch'an* because it's Chinese and not Japanese) lies in the ten oxherding pictures of Master Kuo-an. (Trevor, 1969) My Zen teacher liked to call the ox, the bull (she had been a biologist after all) because she felt it better expressed the wildness of our ungentle nature and the struggles of training (Schloegl, 1977, p. 97). These pictures showed ten distinct stages in training, or gentling the bull.

The **first** picture shows the ceaseless search for the bull, never really missing from the beginning, just unnoticed and neglected. We have felt a sense of incompleteness, that something is missing, our understanding is less than clear. We are thoroughly confused and bewildered. I can always see in my mind's eye my son Toby, then very young, visiting London Zoo. He was captivated not by the elephants or rhinos because they were too large to take in, but by the many sparrows feeding off the picnic crumbs. The social worker is searching for her or himself, seeking some sort of contacting fulfilment. The **second** picture portrays the insistent searcher finding some traces of the bull, but this is just an intellectual grasp, just various ideas – nothing of any depth. The seeker cannot yet distinguish between the genuine and the fake, only the traces and not the substance are located. He or she seeks everywhere and finds real as well as fool's gold, but both glister.

The **third** phase is finding the bull. 'There is no longer a place for the ox (bull) to hide' (Trevor, 1969, p. 9). The seeker becomes completely absorbed by the bull. 'Head on the herdsman collided with the ox (bull). He or she no longer needs to run after the bellowing' (ibid., p. 10). He or she realises that the bull has been on show all the time as with my young son Toby's elephants. The **fourth** phase is catching the bull. It is extremely resistant, long used to going his own wild and ferocious way and eating the sweet grass exactly where and when he wants to. If it is to become gentler and gradually accepting of the herdsman, then a lot of disciplined training is required.

The **fifth** lies in the taming. It rushes all around, trying to escape any attempt at discipline, to get back to grazing the grass and the vast fields. The seeker must begin the gentling process with great skill. This requires complete concentration, through *za zen*, meditation practice so as not to let the mind wander off wilfully. The **sixth** is returning home on the back of the bull, facing towards the business end. The fierce struggle is now over and rider and bull have become one, as they always were except in the delusions of the herdsman.

> *Sitting back to front on the ox (bull) he comes home with a joyful heart,*
> *Wearing a bamboo hat and a straw coat in the evening mist.*
> *Step by step. A cool breeze wafts gently.*
> *The ox (bull) does not waste a glance on the once so alluring grass.'*
>
> (ibid., p. 16)

The **seventh** is forgetting the bull, with only the herdsman remaining. There is no duality in the Dharma, only complete unity. Now the herdsman sits alone – quiet and content. The **eighth** is complete oblivion of both bull and herdsman. 'All worldly desires have fallen away.' There is no attachment even to the Lord Buddha, just getting on with everyday living. (ibid., p. 19).

The **ninth** is returning to the ground and the origin. 'It has been pure from the beginning and there is no dust' (ibid., p. 21). The seeker remains completely undistracted by the transitory delusions of everyday living. The sun shines and the rain falls and all things are contemplated. The **tenth** and final picture is entering the market with open hands. 'He has buried his illuminated nature deep and allows himself to turn off the much-travelled tracks of the venerable sages of old.' There is now no teaching or writing. 'He sometimes enters the marketplace with a hollowed-out gourd or returns to his hut with a staff. He visits the drinking places and fish stalls as he pleases, to awaken the drunkards there to themselves.' (ibid., p. 23).

These *ten stages* tell the story from seeker to herdsman to the disappearance of the bull and then the herdsman, and then finally returning to the original marketplace and disappearing. Students of counselling, social work or whatever start to find themselves out of direct experience of personal incompleteness. He or she goes through this circular search to feel the full power of the bull. Eventually this means living an ordinary life, without wishing to help or change anyone, but out of this non-action comes awakening. But this particular special journey is over-hyped – it is no big deal.

> *When one succeeds in reaching there and returns,*
> *The world is without peculiarity just as it is.*
> *It is rainy and misty on Mount Lu-shan.*
> *The torrent rises high and wide in the River Hsi-chiang.*

(ibid., p. 96)

As Schloegl (1977 p. 21) wrote:

> *Only by becoming truly human is deliverance possible, and only then is conscious awareness of, and conscious co-operation with the life-energy, with the Buddha nature, possible. Delivered from the delusion of I with all its subsidiary delusions, the true human lives and acts in harmony with this nature. In the truly human heart forged by its own endeavour, this energy is reflected as warmth and clarity.*

Living death

So how are we riding the non-existent bull? How can we acquire a smidgen of discipline? Seeing the enormity of my task, the Lord Buddha sent me a highly unlikely spiritual master. My marriage to Althea in 1963 had brought a father-in-law – Leslie. By then his red hair had thinned out and turned to white, atop a stooped figure. He had worked for more than 40 years as an office manager for a London-based yeast firm, except for a five-year break as an inefficient signaller in the war against the Germans.

Our relationship was not at all easy. In his youth he had been a considerable chess player – East End of London champion – and linguist. Now he was a rapidly ageing, nervously restless heavy smoker, but very generous to his new young son-in-law. For example he and his wife paid for our first flat to be built on the top of their bungalow in Buckinghamshire, and later provided us with money towards a mortgage. Each evening he returned late from his Liverpool Street office to the house in rural Buckinghamshire that we all shared. By then he was exhausted, and overly content with alcohol he mostly dozed in front of the TV with his dinner half-finished on a wooden tray.

Each morning on the 8.10 am train from Staines to Waterloo he cascaded inconsequential conversation whilst I tried quietly to read the *Manchester Guardian* (as it was in those far-off days). He was very difficult to follow. His topics jumped all over the place – from domestic life to sport to current affairs and back again – all washed down with a quick dry wit. I regularly got cross but uncharacteristically held my tongue. The silent fuming polished the rough pebbles.

In pursuit of my career, our new family – Stewart had arrived and Toby would follow not long after – split from the in-laws and moved south to Shoreham-by-Sea on the English Channel and then north to Hatfield and Preston in Lancashire. The in-laws followed us as far as Shoreham and wonderfully loving mother-in-law died painfully not long after. So father-in-law and grand-father-in-law (mother-in-law's father) shared a house, not terribly comfortably, until grandfather went into an old people's home and died soon afterwards.

Leslie deteriorated in his early seventies. He had retired early from his job and so gave up the commuting that had provided a disciplined framework for the weekdays. He watched TV, smoked incessantly and went out to the pub. His memory deteriorated. He was less able to look after himself and unsuited to living alone. Neighbours had given a lot of support and felt increasingly overwhelmed. There was a crisis when he wandered along the road in the early hours of one morning. It was decided that he should move the 250 miles north to Preston – an alien land – and share the family home with our two young children. It was a prospect I dreaded.

That was a very difficult experience for all of us for several years. He was extremely forgetful and untidy. It is hard for non-smokers to accept floors covered with ash. Looking after grandpa and the two young children split us in various ways. It was often like having an elderly cuckoo in the nest. Over time he grew even worse and required much greater attention. It was difficult to banish the smell of stale urine from the house. We rarely went out. We almost never invited people to our home. We became very stressed and our own rela-tionships were extremely strained. We felt completely isolated and desolate.

Eventually, in an attempt to gain some relief, we moved him into a separate small flat about a half mile away, close to the main road. Surprisingly, he managed reasonably well for nearly a year and the new arrangement gave us all much more space. Althea visited him, usually several times a day, to provide cooked meals, to do the laundry, and a thousand other practical things such as changing light bulbs.

By that time, he'd developed cataracts on both eyes and had only blurred vision. An operation was arranged at the nearby general hospital. He was supposed to be in for only a few days but things got really bad. He became restless and confused. They transferred him to the geriatric ward, where he gained the label of arteriosclerotic. After a few weeks, with the great pressure on beds, he was sent to a nearby convalescent home, a former isolation hospital and now a glorified short-stay facility for elderly people.

When eventually he returned to the flat, we faced an immediate crisis. He just couldn't manage on his own at all. He wandered around restlessly, not knowing where or even who he was. He lived mostly in the previous decades, imagining that his wife was still alive. He related to people and situations that had long since vanished. Sometimes he was doubly incontinent. He could no longer even make a cup of tea.

One morning he pissed in the lounge and there was shit in the hall. I was raging and boiling inside. I stood right in front of him and wanted to punch him to the floor, kick his stupid smiling face and break both his wrists. I wanted to see him disintegrate into ten thousand pieces, to see him die. He was a stupid useless piece of decaying flesh. I wanted the satisfaction of killing him. I was completely terrified by those immense feelings inside me. I sat down feeling very sick. I'd never felt anything like the power of those feelings. I hated this surge, this overwhelming hatred that seemed much bigger and stronger than me. It was as though an old scab had been painfully scraped off. I wasn't sure sometimes whether I faced my father or my father-in-law.

We were both rapidly losing any tiny residue of dignity and control. We had to call in help. We worked our way through the usual forked and mystifying labyrinth of health and social services. Community psychiatric nurses came and changed light bulbs and made corned beef sandwiches, sometimes with pickle. They seemed to work in a kind of partnership, to have joined a sparse team of people supporting a confused and often unhappy old man. They supported us through action.

When social workers came they seemed different. They never came singly; they came in pairs and on one occasion as a threesome, as if they were going to be mugged. They looked at us and examined, almost prodded from a distance. They were like local government inspectors. They had sheaves of forms and briefcases and were constantly asking questions and filling in those forms. They were minor bureaucrats working for the Social Services Department. They definitely didn't change light bulbs. Mostly they told us what we couldn't have. We couldn't have meals on wheels to ease the situation at lunch times: we lived in the wrong area – if only we had lived two miles further south. We couldn't have a home help to assist in keeping the flat clean, keeping an eye on him, getting the shopping in. It would have helped everyone if we'd lived someplace else, preferably far away.

We kept ringing the area Social Services office to emphasise the crisis and they eventually arrived – usually in couples – to visit. They were 'assessing'. They asked lots of questions, filled in numerous forms and said 'No' to lots of requests. They shook their heads gravely many times and said a great deal about the limits of the existing legislation and did hardly anything. They always said they would contact us again and never did until we ourselves rang the office. One social worker recommended that we write to our MP about the dire situation. That added insult to injury.

There was one interview where I stood in for Althea. At that time I was the director of North West MIND so the issues surrounding confused, elderly, mentally ill people were close to my professional as well as personal interests, although I was rarely able to square them. This youngish, rather officious social worker called at the house. He carried a briefcase full of forms and talked initially of assessment and of the department's problems.

He spoke of practical difficulties. Was father-in-law a health or social services responsibility? There seemed to be a substantial battle going on behind the scenes. We talked very practically and politically for something like 15 minutes – about commodes, wheelchairs, the lack of home help services, possible admission to old people's homes... Then I realised that the conversation had turned into counselling. I was being advised of 'better' ways to cope.

It was subtle blackmail, sometimes not so subtle. As a caring relative I didn't really exist in my own right. I wasn't the client. The single client was and had to be Grandpa, who wasn't a person any more but a series of conditions and syndromes. Both Althea and I were simply adjuncts to him; a means of supporting his infirmity. Althea and I had become unpaid members of a professional team. Without agreement or any discussion, we'd become 'carers'. No one tended to our grief and distress because we weren't clients. We were invisible. We'd have to break down psychiatrically and become clients in our own right to be heard. There was a possibility of real support, but to receive it we had to be cooperative, open and compliant. I had to share my wounds and vulnerabilities to compete effectively with unseen others in the lottery for help.

The third stage in this assessment interview was reached when the counselling turned into basic homespun philosophy. This pompous young professional ended with a few words about his own devout Roman Catholic faith, which apparently sustained him through the stresses of situations like ours and a lot more. Attending Sunday mass was an enriching experience – he recommended it. I was really furious but gave a toothy smile.

Later this experience spurred me on to Old Testament style vengeance. I rang the area social services officer, whom I knew, and threatened retribution. 'We need some action not forms and visits', I said with great power, hardly needing the phone. It didn't help much. Through the post, we received a scruffy list of rest homes on a single sheet of paper. We began a long round of residential enquiries. We located a seemingly suitable home in Southport, but it quickly proved very unsuitable. Within hours they were asking for his removal. He was too infirm, too disturbed, too restless, he required skills and support that they didn't possess. He cost too much. They wanted passive elderly people who could be quietly neglected, not a confused and disturbed old man who needed expensive attention.

After several false starts he ended up in the dreadful back ward of a local psychiatric hospital – the infamous Whittingham, a scandalous mental hospital in the early 1970s but nowadays closed and deserted. The standard of the facilities was low and the support patchy. But it was either his admission or ours. We'd reached the very end of the line after a long four years. We had had a long lesson in discipline. We visited dutifully each weekend. Some staff were welcoming and others openly hostile. Carefully I made some comment about the radio being very loud so we couldn't converse with Dad. The charge nurse responded with a toothy smile: 'You can always take back him home – can't you?'

Now we were abject beggars asking for favours that stirred my immense anger and frustration. They had all the power. They owned him. We were never asked about any of his likes or dislikes; anything of his personal character or history. They knew absolutely nothing about him and didn't feel anything about that lack of knowledge. We had lost all rights by letting him go. We couldn't get any help so long as he remained in the community, not even meals on wheels. When we abandoned him to the total institution, we lost the right to be his closest relatives. He lost his rights of citizenship in becoming a long-stay patient.

Nothing changed much when he was transferred to the Elderly Severely Mentally Ill Unit (ESMI), presumably the brainchild of some deranged mandarin in the deep Whitehall south. The ESMI unit cost megabucks and was space aged with staff battle stations chock-full with electronic switches.

It seemed it could take off to Mars at any moment. There was a day service on the ground floor, and residential facilities on the first and second floors. Excellent views of the cemetery next door were to be had from every window. It would have been very simple to lift the coffins directly over the stone walls.

It was a sanitised hell – completely plastic and unhomely in every detail. It had few human comforts. The staff wore crisp nurse-style uniforms although most were unqualified and untrained. Only the senior staff were qualified nurses. Again we were beggars at the gate; we had no real status and the information system was rudimentary. We visited each Sunday and departed as soon as we decently could. It was hard not to be stifled in such an atmosphere.

He lived a sort of quarter life for several years. He gradually became more and more incoherent, with only very brief flashes of cockney wit, his awareness soon overwhelmed once more by the darkness of confusion. He died amongst strangers, although mercifully, at the last, his lovely daughter Althea was with him, far from anything he or we might call home. For his remaining family, he had really died some years before.

The ESMI unit forced both of us to be strangers to him. We were rarely consulted or involved in any way. The staff took him over; owned the whole of his being. On one level that was a great relief for us after years of suffering; but on another, deeper, level it was a tragedy. Slowly, together we learned to carry the massive guilt of abandonment. I had met a man with whom I ordinarily wouldn't have spent five minutes, but to whom I had gained some mysterious commitment through marriage that I never properly understood and failed to honour.

What are the lessons here? There were immense emotional storms over a number of years. I'm often wrecked on these historical coral reefs, trapped in the anguish and the guilt. I need help, not sermonising. How do I get off; how do I escape back to the open sea and the fresh wind again? 'I must go down to the sea again, the lonely sea and the sky, and all I ask is a tall ship and a star to steer her by. . . .' How do I stay just where I am?

Unintentionality

Can we intend or not intend, and what does that mean? In response to Einstein's famous quip 'God does not play with dice', (Hawking, 1988, p. 66) the physicist Davies responded: 'Our consciousness weaves a route at random along the ever-branching evolutionary pathway of the cosmos, so it is we rather than God who is playing dice' (Hofstadter and Dennett, 1982, p. 48).

Within that confusing framework does it mean anything to have a purpose, to intend? What is the influence of purpose on helping people? If we set out to achieve some objectives/tasks within a professional relationship, what effect does that intention have on the process? Are such intentions usually made explicit? Many 'clients' talk of the value of simple humanity in helping and healing. What does it mean to be 'simply human'? Can it be intended, or is this just a more subtle form of manipulation?

Levi writes of his experiences in Auschwitz concentration camp.

> *I believe that it was really due to Lorenzo that I am alive today; and not so much for his material aid, as for his having constantly reminded me by his presence, by his natural and plain manner of being good, that there still existed a just world outside our own, something and someone still pure and whole, not corrupt, not savage, extraneous to hatred and terror, something difficult to define, a remote possibility of good, but for which it was worth surviving.* (Levi, 1979, p. 127).

He received vital reminders of what it meant to be genuinely human from a giver with no self-consciousness. It seems clear that Lorenzo did not intend the gift. It arose, in Levi's view, out of 'his natural and plain manner of being good'. The Tao Te Ching echoes a similar theme.

> *A 'do-gooder' wants to be seen to be good.*
> *Natural goodness is unconcerned with appearances.*
> *A 'do-gooder' may be endlessly busy,*
> *But there always seems more to be done.*
> *Natural Goodness seems to do nothing,*
> *And good things just happen.*

> (Freke, 1995, p. 76)

Several years ago in a large shopping Mall I watched this scene. About 80 yards in front of me an elderly lady had fallen down an escalator. Her shopping had spilled everywhere. One of her legs was bleeding, and with the escalator still moving there remained other possible dangers. Five or six people, none known to the lady or each other until moments before, burst in to action, forming a collaborative team. A young man pressed the emergency button to stop the escalator; a couple lifted her from the metal stairs, where she was balanced precariously, to the main floor, and someone's coat was placed under her head. A middle-aged man dialled 999 to call an ambulance. A young woman came out from the nearest shop to say they had a first aid kit. Everyone was touched by this experience.

As I came nearer, yet another woman knelt over the elderly 'patient', asked how she was, placed a firm and protective arm on her shoulder and explained that she was an off-duty nurse. The woman seemed a little shaky but unbowed. The gash in her leg wasn't so bad, although there was a lot of blood. The main actors stood around sympathetically, awaiting the arrival of the ambulance. One young man had blood on his jacket from lifting her off the escalator. Another young man and woman collected her spilled shopping and put it all back in the bags. Other people offered help but weren't needed, so effectively had the 'team' performed. And then the experts arrived. The ambulance could be heard some distance off; the paramedics, so familiar from various TV programmes, dressed in medical uniforms carrying special-ist equipment, arrived efficiently and quickly. The helpers melted away or became curious onlookers.

For a few minutes these complete strangers had acted selflessly, had given no thought for themselves. Nobody had thought 'This is no business of mine', or if they had, they had dismissed it and taken responsibility, like the Good Samaritan. Then the middle-aged man looked at his watch and the spell was broken. The young man talked to his girlfriend and they went off, leaving the off-duty nurse in charge. The patient seemed fine and people remembered who they were – an accountant going to a busy company board meeting; a mother collecting her kids; a young woman in love. . . . For a few moments the world had frozen in a compassionate snapshot, but then, as in the marvellous last lines of Larkin's poem *Aubade* the everyday world began once more. The shopping mall accident became an event, to be mused over that evening in front of a score of TV sets or even earlier in two dozen offices. But for a few moments all those ordinary people had behaved extraordinarily, lost in the service of a single distressed other.

> *Meanwhile telephones crouch, getting ready to ring*
> *In locked-up offices, and all the uncaring*
> *Intricate rented world begins to rouse.*
> *The sky is white as clay, with no sun.*
> *Work has to be done.*
> *Postmen like doctors go from house to house.*
>
> (Larkin, 1990)

I was in my twenties and working in Islington, north London. I was at a road junction when down the hill came a baby's pram – you dream of this sort of event as a teenager, a chance to be a hero. A woman was screaming further up the hill. I guessed she was the mother. I reached out my left hand and stopped the pram from going into the road, underneath the wheels of a passing car. The baby was crying. The car stopped, several people gathered around and the mother hurried to her baby. I stood there with no ideas in my head. The mother gathered up her child, pushed the pram past by me and went off into the distance. I came back from the Unborn Mind and immediately felt angry. My heroic nature was unrecognised. A voice inside commanded: 'David – don't be silly.'

It's hard to have none or few expectations of the people, with whom we are working, especially to do it purposively, as we saw from the gestalt drycleaner. Out of our expectations and opinions come desires that they should be this way or that way which can easily become strong pressures on them. Ideals of how they should be can become a silent tyranny. Unconsciously our clients can be pushed and pulled in various directions that suit our ways of being and living. They are remade in our image of how they ought to be, which usually does not succeed, and then they are punished in a thousand subtle and not so subtle ways for their imagined deficiencies.

Often there seem no alternatives to fashionably dominant paradigms. Instead of perceived fluidity, ordinary ways of living seem to come in blocks of ice. Peile (1993, pp.127–34) argues that

> *social workers, clients, and research subjects are all predominantly caught up in the self-deceptive trap of determinism, which blinds each to their own and each other's creative potential and capacities. Social structures have developed that further entrench and protect the deterministic world view.*

Unity
The Mulla Nasrudin saw a troop of horseman approaching him on a deserted road. He became very frightened and his imagination worked overtime. He imagined himself captured and sold as a slave. He ran away and hid in a graveyard, lying down in an open tomb. The honest travellers followed and asked: 'What are you doing in that grave? Can we help you?' 'Just because you ask a question doesn't mean that there is a straightforward answer,' said the Mulla, 'It all depends on your viewpoint. If you must know: I am here because of *you*, and you are here because of *me*.' (Shah, 1966, p. 16) Well how very true, although I'm not sure exactly what it means.

Of course the Mulla is making fun of us, of himself – as well as of the travellers. He makes us look at the habit we have of looking at part of something; slicing things up and almost forgetting the whole picture. He is chiding us for even considering that different parts can resemble the whole. Even if we put all the fragments together again, there is still a gestalt, an intimate relationship between him and those friendly travellers, as well as some thoughts about neurotic paranoid delusions.

Studies of homeless people in Romania give this sense of wholeness. On various visits to Bucharest to study homelessness, I saw a considerable number of isolated and disabled individuals, especially around the Gara du Nord railway station, living in the heating ducts above the metro. These were the scattered and shabby victims of various oppressive institutions, such as the infamous orphanages. With the help of two young interpreters I talked to a number of individuals, most fairly young, struggling hard to survive against huge odds. Mostly they sniffed very cheap oven-cleaner fluid out of plastic bags, and they made small amounts of cash from begging and portering jobs around the small market and the railway station.

Whilst sitting in a cheap café interviewing a young man, we were challenged aggressively by a guy called Florin. He demanded to know what we were up to. We had been seen around by some other homeless people. He was well dressed with considerable presence and dignity. After a few tense moments, realising that we were researchers and not police spies, he sat down, drank some coffee and talked. He was the king of the beggars in that zone. He organised a community of people living together with various segments in different parts of a vast heating system. They defended themselves against other homeless groups from different parts of Bucharest. 'We are the best.' There were several section leaders with responsibility for job allocation and welfare.

Now, instead of seeing these young people as socially alienated, I saw them as part of a cohesive group that in many ways looked out for each other. The various aid agencies ignored or simply didn't know about these support networks and dealt with the individuals only. They gave clothing to this person, food to that individual. Florin opened my eyes to see at least a tiny part of the whole.

Bananas in Bucharest

He crouched in the crowded Metro carriage
reciting the Lord's prayer in his own language
'Hallowed be thy name . . .'
in all the dust, bustle and noise –
followed by the suggested reward,
small dirty hand outstretched
from the seven year old body,
'Give us our daily bread. . . .'

Our eyes met briefly,
I had no small change or bread
so he left for greener pastures
until I remembered the bananas
in the shopping bag
and offered a yellow fruit
delighting the dark brown eyes
scurried to a far corner
like a small squirrel.

The banana was a mystery,
biting the top hesitantly
with no knowledge of peeling
and then still puzzled
the train stopped
hurried to the next carriage
to chant 'Thy will be done on earth
as it is in Heaven . . .'
once more to busy passengers,
whose hearts were already fixed
on the comforts of home.

We contain such an incredible diversity inside our minds – an infinite number of characters in the restless search for coherent identity. Many of our identities are openly at war with one another. They can barely tolerate contact, and when and if they do, explosions can follow. We saw that in the earlier story of the fierce German shepherd dog. Thich Nat Hanh talks about struggling with our anger and creating a battlefield in the mind. 'If you struggle in that way, you do violence to yourself. If you cannot be compassionate to yourself, you will not be able to be compassionate to others. When we get angry, we have to produce awareness: 'I am angry. Anger is in me. I am anger.' (Hanh, 1982, p.40).

It is immensely hard for us to love ourselves whilst feeling that we're not good enough by an immensely long measure. I know that feeling so well. We tend to turn everything, including personal growth, into a military campaign. We can easily use the gentle and loving words of Thich Nhat Hanh to beat ourselves even further and harder. Any spiritual instruction can be converted into a rod with which to beat ourselves rather than use as an awakening stick.

Chapter 7
Uniqueness not Individualism

Can you value your uniqueness, as part of the Whole?
Be subtle as breath, and supple as a baby?
Be a polished Mirror, reflecting Truth perfectly?

(Freke, 1995, p. 44)

Our struggle to be individuals, different from others, has been well noted in these pages. It is extremely socially valued to be distinct, above the herd rather than below it. But our desperate struggle to become distinct can result in us looking and sounding similar. We wear the same sorts of fashionable colours and styles; even deviate from the norm in similar ways; think the same sorts of ideas, driven by contemporary, powerful social and economic forces. Even when we do manage to be special, seemingly in some way 'unique', it turns out to be distinctive only in the way that many others are. The woman at the Ascot horse races discovers that a dozen others are wearing the same dress and hat. She is mortified; her great day in the royal enclosure absolutely ruined. Striving hard to gain accretions – like thousands of barnacles on a ship's hull – serves only to warp her true nature.

We feel that being 'special' involves becoming important, acquiring things and designer labels on our clothes. We can become like scouts and girl guides – skills in cooking, pathfinding, sailing, knot tying, tent pitching; invisible badges all over the clothes. 'I'm a qualified counsellor, hold a degree in . . ., can mend a lawn mower, fix a car. . . . I'm a wife, mother, car driver, recently went to a garden party at Buckingham Palace . . .' What have all these 'things'and 'roles'got to do with who we really are? Do they add up to a hill of beans? The waters of *Tao Te Ching* wash our transient lives and achievements, certificates and competencies right down to the sea, leaving not a trace.

This striving for special individuality and distinctiveness is not healing but sickness. The healing doesn't lie in accentuating separateness but in coming together.

The reason for the Buddhist community life (Sangha) is inherent in the nature of the Buddha's teaching. We have seen that this teaching consists of diagnosis and prescription: diagnosis of the human malaise as consisting essentially of the disease of individualism, and prescription for its cure as consisting primarily of the undermining or erosion of the notion that individuality is something permanent and of great

119

importance. It is in the life of the Sangha that the prescription can
most effectively be applied. Here is the community of being which
comes into existence when the walls of individuality are completely
and permanently broken down. And here too, are found the optimum
conditions for those who are seeking to achieve that state of life and
consciousness where individuality is no more, but who have not yet
arrived at that state. (Ling, 1976, p.152)

We may desire but don't need this pursuit of individuality. We may desire
independence but thirst and hunger for interdependence, finding harmony in
working and collaborating with others. We need an active fellowship – a
sense of union with others, as the Buddha suggested, that may come over the
internet or more likely through ordinary conversations, cuddles and laughs
from those intimate to us, both geographically and emotionally.

Of the many threats to the building of community, one comes from the belief
that we have nothing much to learn from the past, based firmly on the illusion
of progress. It worships everything that is modern, combined with a profound
disrespect for our grandmothers and grandfathers, either literally or in developing professional disciplines. For example the study of prehistory teaches
us that our ancestors were much more accomplished than we ever imagined.
Too much preoccupation with modernity can lead us to look to the future and
rarely back into the past. We need vision in both directions – past and future –
as well as the clearly focused skills to survive in the present moment.

Uniqueness
A Zen teacher who ran a bakery employing homeless people just outside
New York commented:

One of the most popular pastries we baked was ... a dense chocolate
torte ... it turned out to be delicious and special. Around that time, we
hired a professional baker to help us increase our efficiency – and he
made a few changes in the way we prepared our Godiva chocolate
torte. Almost immediately, we got a call from the people at Godiva, and
they said, 'What's happened?' In fact it was good. But it was good the
way any other chocolate torte was good. It was no longer special ...
Experts can be useful ... but ... we had to learn to keep our uniqueness
and style.... (Glassman and Fields, 1996, p.68).

This outlines the tension between our drive to be special and our original face, or
as Bankei would have called it, our unborn mind. The top confectionery expert

on chocolate tortes came to give advice, just like any expert in making over deficient psyches. He did this job well, analysing and reconstructing the process of cake making so that the new product was uniformly excellent. He looked at every tiny segment of a complex operation in great professional detail. The brand new chocolate torte was launched and delivered to the shops, amid great pride, glossy brochures and the loud fanfare of trumpets. Everyone was delighted.

However there was a great problem in the shops. The purchasers of the new torte compared it adversely with the previous, so-called inferior version. Their mouths and stomachs were fine judges. It wasn't that the original torte had been better or worse, but that it had been 'unique'and the new version was uniform and standardised. The new and delicious torte was like everyone else's – mouthwatering, but delicious in the same way as everyone else's. You could buy this sort of torte in most discerning confectioners, almost anywhere. The original might have been 'less perfect', whatever that means, but it had been a definite reflection of that particular bakery, in a way that the new one was not. It was a direct expression of the expert's work.

This was the result of conscientiously and eternally striving to be better. To make perceived improvements is an important aspect of human striving, but we can get hemmed in with fantasies of improvement, as Feynman might have noted. They can be self-incarcerating and claustrophobic. They can reject the natural flow of the chocolate, with all its quirky, incalculable outcomes, in favour of something much more calculated and planned which is content with agreed standards, measured dessert spoons and regulations.

This is an almost irresistible movement from the scruffy to the slick. The old torte-making process in that particular bakery was scruffy and large elements were virtually unmeasured, based on guesswork. The new system, cleverly designed by the confectionery expert was slick. Everything from start to finish was completely standardised and measured.

Another early Taoist text says:

> '*Deep thinking generates knowledge,*
> *Idleness and carelessness generate worry.*
> *Cruelty and arrogance generate resentment.*
> *Worry and greed generate illness.*
> *When illness reaches a distressing degree, you die.*

When you think about something and don't let go of it,
Internally you will be distressed, externally you will be weak.
Do not plan things out in advance
Or else your vitality will ceded its dwelling.

(Roth, 1999, p. 84)

There is no need to search to be unique, we are already. My Mam said frequently, almost always of other women, 'She's no better than she should be'. I'm not exactly sure what that meant, except it was very dismissive. The drive for psychological and even spiritual betterment, as with chocolate tortes, can take us away from our original face. We can become standardised, similar in artificial ways to most others. Not only do we end up wearing the same jeans or chinos, but our naked souls are clothed similarly. Our essential 'vitality'as the *Nei-yeh* Taoist text has it, comes from being wholly and fully who we really are. Christ of the Gospels talks of 'living more abundantly'. 'Worry and greed generate illness', and an increasing craving to be better can easily be a denial, a fundamental lack of acceptance of who we really are. That sort of craving can never be satisfied by hungry ghosts.

Recipes

Nowadays our TV screens are packed full of DIY gurus and cookery experts. There's no end to the demand for this sort of basic entertainment. One extremely popular cook is like a pharmacist, a domestic scientist, presiding over a large kitchen and measuring with extraordinary care the various ingredients for the dish. Her culinary precision is remarkable and she uses a traditional pedagogic style. You know that her instructions should be followed exactly and will always end up with a delicious meal. It feels as though you're sitting in a Royal Institute lecture theatre at Christmas, observing a great technician at work.

Yet another popular TV cook travels abroad a lot and has on hand vast amounts of cheap red wine to flavour various dishes and sauces. Much of this wine goes down his own throat. In great contrast to the pedagogue, this chef throws handfuls of herbs and this and that into various simmering saucepans. You don't feel lectured at all, not at all like a small errant child, but part of a hastily arranged party, where the guests become increasingly inebriated and begin to dance. In one kitchen the stress is on the goals, and in the other its on the whole enjoyable process. In one kitchen processing food is an exact science, in the other flamboyant fun.

One experience is of very formal learning, where my admiration of the cooking teacher grows and grows. But afterwards, I don't feel like cooking or that I've gained increased confidence, or even feel the slightest bit hungry. It all feels rather like painting a Rembrandt by numbers. With the second cook, it's all great comedy, although I'm not sure what he's doing or where we're going. It's not an ascetic experience but sensual. After all this is not medicine, but eating and drinking. I could throw this and that into any old pan and it would taste reasonable, especially if I drank sufficient alcohol.

With the famous pedagogue I can be confident that her recipe will *always* work out correctly but it will never really belong to me. It will remain firmly hers. Like the chocolate cake, it will be excellent but always uniformly excellent, nothing genuinely distinctive and unique. With the second chef, it will never be his, it would always belong to me – whether edible or not, it will have a unique, un-uniform quality. Every time this dish is made, it will taste different.

The second chef passed on to me via the TV something of the joys of cooking, the real process of preparing food. Although impossible to follow, even when sober, he took a whole liberating process and communicated it, as all great teachers rather than technicians do. He captured its whole spirit.

Social work teaching strikes me as much the same. Many of us give the students a series of diagrams and carefully organised strategies from handbooks that look more like car repair manuals – year on year. Each particular part is exactly described – dissections of empathy, projecting warmth and accurate feedback – but it bears very little relationship to the whole activity. We haven't communicated the essence – any of the warmth and fun – in our presentation.

Buddha of St Martins

I've been fortunate to meet several great teachers in my social work career, although I didn't usually realise they were great until a long time afterwards. One early encounter, whilst working with homeless people underneath Hungerford Bridge, was with the author Norman Croucher who had written *The King of the Shin Kickers*. He was the king of this ancient Cornish sport because he'd had both legs taken off by a train when drunk. Ever tried kicking the shins of a man with metal legs?

My first practical lesson in social work took place at St Martins-in-the-Fields. Of course I had read some related books and articles, mostly of the sickly sentimental 'I rescued the homeless' type; and attended several relevant lectures and seminars, but those were simply words and this was so much more. There was the world of difference between going to the zoo to watch the big cats sleeping and actually wrestling with them, feeling their sharp claws and teeth on your flesh. Although my teenage years sleeping rough in London had involved some direct wrestling with the tigers.

I was visiting the beautiful church in noble Trafalgar Square, a stone's throw from the Van Goghs and Cezannes in the National Gallery and very close to my own office underneath Hungerford Bridge. Down some steep steps was a grotty social care centre for homeless people, presided over by Reg, whom I'd presumed on several previous meetings to be affable but bumbling. The centre, which had a strong nineteenth-century odour, gave bus tickets and small amounts of cash to various itinerants.

Reg let me sit in on brief interviews. It was fascinating to see him at work. There was the usual long series of depressing encounters, an eternal Indian file of the disabled, the elderly and what used to be called before the war 'the feckless'. These people were 'down on their luck'. Many were old soldiers, British Legion types, never adjusting to civvy street, whilst others emerged periodically from assorted prisons and mental hospitals into the smog and busy traffic. Reg dealt with them in a limp, courteous and priestly style. He seemed devoid of any organisation. He had a natural gift for anarchy, of the 'large piles of files all over the floor' variety. He gave the many downtrodden guests some quality time, whereas I was more brisk and business-like, operating on piecework and strongly influenced by my idea of what constituted professional skills – that mostly meant being a bit of a bastard.

I vividly recall one encounter. The man was in his early thirties, wearing dirty work trousers and a scruffy T shirt. 'I'm a time-served carpenter by trade, mostly working on buildings. Split up with my wife some years ago, she was always difficult to live with, and never seen the two bairns since. Just come in to King's Cross from Birmingham on the train. Left my carpentry tools in the left luggage office so I could look for work. After a couple of days of looking, I've found work with Laings in Lambeth and start work tomorrow morning at 6. I need £2 to pay to get the tools out of the station. And I don't have a penny piece. I'll pay you back in a few weeks.'

Reg listened carefully and gravely. After a few more questions and many serious nods of the head, he got out a battered tin cash box and handed over two scruffy pound notes. The man bowed his head, uttered repeated thank yous and left hurriedly, as if Reg might suddenly change his mind. I was astounded. At my welfare office for the homeless at the other end of Northumberland Avenue, he wouldn't have got a brass farthing. He'd have failed the 'deserving' test.

Reg turned to me: 'Well what did you think of that man and his story?'

'I though it was a completely preposterous pack of lies. With those unblemished hands he's no carpenter or builder. You can't get in to King's Cross station from Birmingham by train anyway. He's got a strong Scots accent, probably from the Glasgow area and has been in London some months at least, probably living in a Sally Army hostel. The money is obviously going on the drink right at this very moment.'

'Yes – you are completely right. I can't disagree. He's probably half drunk already.'

'Then why did you give him the £2 if you knew the story was false?'

'Who else in London is he going to fool with such a stupid story? He'll probably starve to death.'

Being intensely full of myself, arrogant and stupid to boot, it took me many years to work on that simple story. It wouldn't let me go. It stuck in my mind like a piece of grit in an oyster. It wouldn't go away. I'm not sure there is any real moral. Morals – drawing out the underlying message – were never the stock in trade of Bankei types. They just got on with ordinary living. The homeless man's story was almost certainly grossly inaccurate but somehow nevertheless true. Reg was a guru who had almost disappeared, forgotten to teach. He had deep saddle sores from too much riding on the backs of bulls.

The emphasis in work with the homeless in those days – and today – was on the great split between the 'deserving' and the 'undeserving', finding out whether you were of 'good character'. If you were of good moral status, then you deserved to be helped; if not, then there was always the workhouse. So the resources were given for presenting good illusions, putting on an attractive charade.

Reg revealed the mirage nature of this – nobody deserves or doesn't deserve, whatever that might mean. Did the Good Samaritan ask for the bona fides of the injured traveller, or even references? He was much more generous than that. He just helped him up onto his beast and paid for his care at the inn, not a passport or social security benefit voucher in sight. A colleague once told me that a forensic social worker, on hearing the Good Samaritan parable, always asked what had happened to the robbers! 'Those poor devils – they need some help and support.'

Rosie's dog

Rosie, a young woman with learning difficulties in her early twenties, had recently been discharged from a long-stay hospital and wanted a dog for her twenty-third birthday. It was her heart's desire. Why? We can only make guesses. Perhaps it was some great symbol of freedom, a celebration of her escape from the grim institution, but she hungered badly for a dog – an ordinary mongrel. 'Please can I have a dog for my birthday?' It seemed a reasonable request.

But unfortunately she had only exchanged one kind of institution for another. She now lived in a staffed group home, run by a large voluntary organisation. The staff wanted to help but the hypothetical mongrel presented huge organisational difficulties. The opinion of the other residents must be taken into account. How would it affect their lives? Perhaps some of them might be allergic to canine fur. Others might not like dogs. There was the whole democratic process to go through, including the views of the staff who had to work there every day. Could she look after this animal? If not, who would take on the responsibility, and was it fair on them? After all dogs are not just for Christmas, but for life. Who would take financial responsibility for any necessary vet's bills when her social security income was so low? What did the complex risk-assessment processes have to say? What if one of the residents was bitten – would the existing household insurance cover it? The process was absolutely endless. There was always yet another steep hurdle.

After two interminable staff meetings the problem was referred ever upwards. Nobody wanted to accept responsibility for this truly awesome decision. At regional office level it became an issue of hygiene, as well as one of endangering the security of the group home through the construction of a dog or cat flap. Various senior officers discussed this endlessly, as well as the implications for fire regulations. What were the regulations about the size and construction of various sorts of door flap? How could the organisation ensure that the builder was adequately insured? Hundreds of pounds was spent, enough to buy a Crufts champion, without any clear decision. National headquarters were asked for guidance.

The whole process took more than five months. Her birthday came and went, and so did Christmas. The file on the canine request grew thicker and thicker, to phone directory size. Phone calls and meetings proliferated. Just before the referral to the United Nations, a good old-fashioned English compromise was reached, balancing the least danger with the greatest acceptability. One evening Rosie came home extremely tired from the adult training centre and was introduced to the home's newest inmate. She passed it by without a break in her step, showing unerring zoological accuracy: 'That's not a dog. It's a cat.'

All those intelligent and professional staff, employed by a caring organisation, were completely unable to respond accurately to the uniqueness of Rosie's desire for a dog. They couldn't recognise the incessant yearning she had for some canine company, that it wasn't remotely like the desire for a cat. She wanted something to train, to take for walks, to throw sticks into the far distance and have some chance they might be brought back. No cat could do all of that.

It wasn't because staff didn't care – they spent thousands of hours trying to square the circle. It wasn't because they couldn't tell the difference between dogs and cats – at least two of them were dog owners. They had also clearly understood, just how important having a dog, as opposed to having a cat, was for Rosie. They had breakfast with her every day, they accompanied her to the local shops. The juggernaut system they operated just wouldn't permit an accurate and sensible decision. Overall guidelines and general principles had to be adhered to. Rosie's choice was only one of any number of items that had to go into the service spin-dryer. All these items had to be taken into account, resulting in a stupid and unsatisfactory compromise, made principally by distant people who were completely unable to recognise the uniqueness of either the hypothetical dog or Rosie.

Again we see how the services are trying to be slick rather than scruffy, erring towards yang and neglecting yin. Efficiency and best value are the bywords. So the dog gets tippexed out and the cat brought purring in. Each step in this long and expensive process is very sensible and coherent, but somehow – largely unintentionally – returns the requested dog into a cat. Every single segment of that essential uniqueness, which Reg taught so well, is ironed out.

Bankei
We've met the seventeenth-century Japanese Zen Master Bankei several times already. He brought to Zen practice an earthy freshness that still breathes through the stories, which even three centuries on still contain an immense vitality. He left no written expositions of his teachings and gave

strict orders that nobody else was to reduce them to writing. Nevertheless his students were disobedient and did record his teachings, in particular about the 'Unborn'.

Take this comment from one sermon:

> *What we call a 'thought' is something that has already fallen one or more removes from the living reality of the Unborn. If you priests would just live in the Unborn, there wouldn't be anything for me to tell you about it, and you wouldn't be listening to me. But because of the unbornness and marvellous illuminative power inherent in the Buddha mind, it readily reflects all things that come along and transforms itself into them, thus turning the Buddha-mind into thought.* (Waddell, 1984, p.34–5)

And from another:

> *You should all listen to my words as if you were newly born this very day. If something's on your mind, if you have any preconception, you can't really take in what I say. But if you listen as if you were a newborn child, it'll be like hearing me for the first time. Since there's nothing in your mind, you can take it right in, grasp it even from a single word, and fully realize the Buddha's Dharma.* (ibid., 1984, p. 63).

But his main lessons are not to be found in the formality of sermons in the temples but rather, like Christ, in the way he lived. During one of his retreats, a student was caught stealing. Others reported it to him and asked for the student's expulsion. Bankei ignored their demand. Later the student was caught stealing again and once more Bankei ignored their request for expulsion. The other students were angry and drew up a petition asking for the thief to be sent away, otherwise they would leave. Bankei read the petition and called everyone before him:

> *You are wise brothers. You know what is right and what is not right. You may go somewhere else to study if you wish, but this poor brother does not even know right from wrong. Who will teach him if I do not? I'm going to keep him here even if all the rest of you leave.' A torrent of tears cleaned the face of the brother who'd stolen. All desire to steal had vanished.* (Brandon, in Claxton, 1986, p. 241).

My favourite story is about hecklers at one of Bankei's lectures. Two students of another teacher were angry when their master lost all his students because they went to hear Bankei talk. They stood on the edge of the crowd and heckled. 'Our teacher can do magic. He can make the clouds move and bring the sunshine. What magic can you do?' Bankei responded: 'It may be that your old fox can do these things but my magic is that when I'm hungry I eat, when thirsty I drink.'

Now that's what I call extremely powerful stuff. It leaves everyone just breathless. He could join any spiritual Magic Circle anywhere in the world with tricks like that. The message was so direct and clear, almost brutal – give up this intense yearning for the mysterious and delectable, live with the world as it genuinely is. See and delight in the ordinary magic and miracles everywhere around you. If these two poor stooges, the hecklers, had even one shred of wisdom, they'd have left their tired old fox and simply followed Bankei, but I don't think they did. I bet they stayed close to their cloud mover. They were looking up in the air for intoxicating conjuring, not for immensely skilful ways of living. Staring upwards, quite soon they would get their sandals all covered in dog shit.

> *No matter how many different thoughts arise, let them remain right where they are. Don't give thought even to what you may find delightful. You mustn't make your one mind into two. If your mind is always set like this, it won't think about what is good and what is not good. It won't think it should not think about such things, or that it should cease to think about them, and therefore thoughts of good and bad cease naturally. The same is true of displeasure and pleasure, which are both merely bred from your self-centredness.* (Waddell, 1984)

Bankei didn't give starving people photographs of loaves of bread. He gave them real loaves so that they could eat their fill. He didn't deal in complicated ideologies and paradigms, but suggested directly what they might do about their perceived problems. He was the direct expression of the Buddha nature, the unborn mind.

On the day of his death the monastery bell began to toll. A young monk coming out of the main gate spoke to a blind beggar who had sat outside for many years. 'The great teacher is dead' said the young monk. 'I'd guessed that. He'd been ill for quite a while' said the beggar, 'He was a really great man. When you're blind you must listen more carefully to the sound of people's voices. Sometimes you can hear that although people say they are sad their voice sounds glad; and sometimes when they say they're glad they sound sad. But with Bankei, in all the years I heard his voice, every time he said he was sad, he was only sad, and every time he said he was glad, he was only glad.'

Empty Boats

I had longed to sail in small boats for most of my life. Brought up close to the sea as a small boy I had watched the boats – both large and small – leaving and coming into the mouth of the busy River Wear. I had stood close to the beloved Saxon church of St Peters, forever associated with the Venerable Bede of Monkwearmouth. I finally learned to sail when close to 50 years old. In the beginning it was sometimes frightening, especially when the water got rough. But after some time I even enjoyed capsizing in the nearly freezing waters of Ullswater in my beloved Lake District. The whole experience is a joy – the strength of a force-six wind; the sound of the sails and sheets; the feeling of the waves. And then, only rarely but always memorable, the emptiness of the small boat, in my case a Topper. For a few moments, there was the wind coming through the gaps in the mountains and the boat and the sailor had somehow merged.

It is clear that – two and half centuries ago – Chuang Tzu, the Taoist, also enjoyed boats, either as an observer or as a sailor, because he used them as a powerful metaphor.

If a man is crossing a river
And an empty boat collides with his own skiff,
Even though he be a bad tempered man
He will not become very angry.
But if he sees a man in the boat,
He will shout at him to steer clear.
If the shout is not heard, he will shout again,
And yet again, and begin cursing.
And all because there is someone in the boat.
Yet if the boat were empty,
He would not be shouting, and not angry.

If you can empty your own boat
Crossing the river of the world,
No one will oppose you,
No one will seek to harm you.

(Merton, 1965, p. 114–5)

I'm even stupid enough to get angry at empty boats. I can get furious at an errant hammer or spanner that doesn't fit or refuses to serve its function. I've always lived in a world where inanimate objects gang up on me, getting ready to ambush. Once I recall capsizing a small sailing dinghy – an

Enterprise, with its blue sails – just by boarding it carelessly. I was so furious with myself that I lost my spectacles in the shallow water through further inattention. Steam burst from my ears.

Chuang Tzu was writing about our projections and expectations. If we see another person in a boat, we develop a whole series of ideas about how they are supposed to think and behave. We assume they have control and operate under the very same principles as we do. Reality may not be like that at all. Whereas if the boat is empty, like the scores of abandoned punts on the River Cam, near where I live, then we don't make any such assumptions.

Imagine that you have an enemy. Someone tells you that he let some people down by not turning up to give a talk. Just imagine the response: 'Well I have to say, he's that sort of person. We have found him to be totally unreliable. He does what he wants to do in the way he wants to do it.' You already had an extremely poor picture of this person and the information just received fits this.

Now suppose this person is a close friend – imagine the very different response: 'This is not at all typical. He must have been sick or had some accident. I can't understand it. We've always found him to be utterly reliable.' On the one hand, when the person is someone we don't like we find the example fits with what we've experienced – the mind-set of the person. On the other, when it's someone we do like we find it incomprehensible and alien to our picture of him. The boat is full both ways!

When I was ordained as a Zen Buddhist monk, I undertook to practice 16 precepts. Most of them were totally impossible, for example the Three Treasures:

> *Be one with the Buddha.*
> *Be one with the Dharma.*
> *Be one with the Sangha.*

But some are hard both to practice and not to practice. I inherited from my Mam the regrettable tendency to be overly critical. She would carve up a neighbour like a surgeon with a laser. When I once appeared on the TV programme *Panorama*, I rang her up from London with pride. 'What did you think?' She responded: 'You let us all down. What are they going to think of us here in the north-east when you go on a TV programme without a tie?' She was a wondrous pricker of hubris.

She loved her daughter-in-law (my wife Althea) greatly and you could tell because although she never ever praised her, she never ever criticised her either.

So the most difficult of the ten grave precepts for me links with that empty Taoist boat: 'Do not elevate yourself by criticising others.'

That's so very hard for me to practice. I'm really familiar with the ten thousand traps that it is heir to, especially the arrogance and stupidity of raising oneself high above others, feeling that you're in some way better. Although in my heart, most of the time I feel not better, but much worse than others. This habitual posture is an expression of the very next grave precept – 'Do not be stingy'. Stinginess reflects a lack of awareness, generosity and compassion towards others. Again it concerns the Taoist empty boat and all the projections that arise from the network of expectations. I should wash my mouth out with carbolic soap every single time I break that precept, except it would be very expensive and do disastrous things to my digestive system!

Good old Bankei knew how it was.

> *I tell my students and those of you coming regularly here to the temple: 'Be stupid!' Because you've got the dynamic function of the marvellously illuminating Buddha Mind, even if you get rid of discriminative understanding, you won't be foolish. So, all of you, from here on, be stupid! Even if you're stupid, when you're hungry, you'll ask for some tea; when it gets warm, you'll put on thin, light clothes, and when it gets cold, you'll put on more clothes. As far as your activities of today are concerned, you're not lacking a thing! With people who are clever, there are sure to be a great many shortcomings. To have transcended those clever people whom all the world holds in great esteem is what's meant by 'stupidity'. There's really nothing wrong with being a blockhead!*
> (Haskel, 1984, p. 80)

Funeral

What is unique about us? When all our roles and other accretions are stripped away and our so-called achievements are no more – with what does death leave us? Bill's long-suffering wife came to my home early one Sunday morning. She had been crying all night. Her tale began rather hesitantly and then became more fluent. 'You'll remember Bill. You met him at some party and he came to visit you several times.' I recalled him well – an awkward, self-opinionated middle-aged man with an extremely chequered career. He'd left many jobs – fruit picker, postal worker, taxi driver – just before he was sacked. We'd had several fierce arguments about the nature of the universe, whether there was life on other planets, about truth... Mostly I enjoyed those arguments but his boss, a former Roman Catholic priest whom I knew well, was not so pleased. He worked in a group home for people with learning difficulties who had recently been discharged from long-stay hospitals. The serious question was, who had the greatest need – he or the residents. Bill was always late for his shift, due to regular drinking bouts.

He was 'pissed off' with his boss, assessed as 'an emotionally constipated bastard'. Bill's diagnosis was probably accurate but it didn't help the smooth running of the shift system. His boss's diagnosis – 'Bill has an ego the size of the Royal Festival Hall and an authority problem to match' – was probably on the ball; they were both shrewd judges of horse flesh if it wasn't their own. I first met Bill at a social event the Christmas before last. He was a larger than life character, drinking gallons of cheap beer and brandy, taking numerous pills, having affairs with assorted colleagues and discovering the occupational disciplines of life in extensive conflict with enormous passions. For Bill, this resulted in a major crisis every year or two.

'You'll have heard that Bill died on Tuesday.' I'd heard on the extensive grapevine that Bill had staggered back late at night from the off-licence, presumably already tanked up. Slaloming across a busy main road, he had been hit violently by a car that hadn't stopped, probably because the driver had been over the alcohol limit himself. 'Well he was a Buddhist. He read a lot of books on Zen and Tibetan Buddhism. I want you to conduct his funeral.' It was a considerable surprise that he was Buddhist. He always seemed a straightforward agnostic. Did reading a few books make you something? It seemed churlish to argue about theological brands, particularly when the object of the discussion was already dead, or at least in between rebirths.

Sometimes I almost forgot my ordination as a Zen Buddhist monk, with the power to conduct funerals, weddings and the like. That time back in 1982 in Los Angeles, my head shaved with a cut-throat razor by a former Harwell rocket scientist; beautifully attired in a white kimono by the abbot of the Zen Centre; belt fastened with velcro (at what point in their long history did they start on velcro?); soon covered in long black medieval robes, tripped over regularly. My naked head bowed to Japanese chanting; the tinkling bells, the overwhelming scent of sweet incense caused a coughing fit and everyone in the packed temple laughed, including my wife. Most of the following year, I regularly wore long black robes. I didn't like the reactions. People responded very stiffly so I put them in the cupboard and got on with the difficult business of being a Buddhist monk in mufti.

I slowly savoured Bill's wife's request. Had her husband's sudden demise slightly unhinged her obviously stable personality? Not only had I never presided over a Buddhist funeral, I had never even attended one. Surely she couldn't be serious. How could I conduct any sort of funeral? To my great surprise, almost shock, I spoke words of agreement. It would take place at 1 pm the next Tuesday. 'What do you want me to say in the funeral address?' 'Tell the truth about him. No nonsense.' Easier said than done – exactly what is true about anyone? But I knew what she meant. There is a convention in newspaper obituaries that only saints die; sinners live forever. A journalist friend killed herself recently and the *Guardian* obituary never mentioned suicide. We needed to speak of his Unborn Mind, the essential nature of the man without any gloss.

The following morning the phone started to ring. First it was the funeral director. What were Buddhist procedures? Could I write them down? Shortly afterwards it was the crematorium. Were there Buddhist hymns that could be played during the service? They were anxious to get tapes for the sound system. People were nervous and confused. We were leaving behind carefully rehearsed scripts.

I began three days of preparation, ringing around his friends. Some were grieving deeply; others were getting on with life. I needed a picture of him as a living breathing person. It was a fairly raunchy and chaotic picture. He drank a great deal; womanised extensively; smoked much dope, mixed with a variety of other drugs; battled with all authorities at all from the Inland Revenue to the police and his gentle boss; and had, in between times, shown great chunks of captivating compassion – a latterday Falstaff. I made copious notes and discussed the eulogy and the service in detail with his wife at a second meeting. She seemed happy with the arrangements

I consulted various books on forms of funeral. Nothing was suitable. The service schedules were all too Japanese for our northern English town. I found a tape of Japanese bamboo flute music – *shakuhachi* – for the worried man at the crematorium. It sounded suitably oriental and dirge-like. If I was to play the fool in front of a hundred plus guests, I'd do it medieval Japanese style. There wouldn't be many samurais present.

The chant for 'unexpected misfortunes' in the Buddhist services book looked promising. There are few greater unexpected misfortunes in life and death than being mown down by a 'hit and run' driver. I started to rehearse. I managed to get a smidgen of that deep-throat sound that Roshi produced effortlessly. The Zen rumour was that young monks practised chanting in front of waterfalls 'until their throats were broken'. I hadn't enough time and the nearest substantial waterfall was 50 miles north in the Lake District.

Suddenly it was the day. I arrived early to prepare – put on the wooden sandals; dressed in the white kimono tied with the velcro belt and the long, black, flowing robes over the top; lit the incense sticks; handed over the flute music tape. . . . More than a hundred gathered: two wives (one ex-); assorted friends and mistresses from work; drinking companions; brothers and sisters; his weeping mother; even a few firm enemies and rather more to whom he owed money; and the crematorium staff, who had never seen a Buddhist funeral, but neither had I. All attention was focused on me, presumably the only person who knew what was happening.

I welcomed people, explaining the service to an eerie silence. My voice came and went in waves, trying to sound confident. 'We'll begin with Japanese music, followed by chanting; followed by a short talk about our friend Bill; then more chanting and a period of silence. The service will begin and end with the sound of this meditation bell.' After the beautifully wistful *shakuhachi* music faded away, I waited for a moment and then began a deep rhythmical chant from back of my throat. The Japanese sounds came pouring into this very Christian chapel of rest. Finishing chanting, I talked slowly of Bill.

'All of us knew Bill. That's why we're here. Not primarily to feel sorrow at his death, although most are grieving, but richly to celebrate his life – who he was and what he did in his uniqueness. He wasn't a saint by a long way. He was an ordinary man with more than his fair share of desires leading a life good in parts and with some great difficulties in others. He had a chequered career - lots of different jobs from bookmaker to postman, from supermarket manager to travelling salesman. He lived life abundantly.

Many will know of his drink and drugs problem. He struggled over many years to kick alcohol and get off dope. Many will know he felt a great failure as a father to his five children. Many more will know that he had intimate relationships with a number of women. It is not our part to judge him here but to tell the truth. The truth is that he worked with people with disabilities; that he read widely and thought deeply; that he wondered a lot about the nature of life and the planet; that he could be difficult and bloody minded; but that there was a great mixture of joy and suffering deep within him. In other words, he was much like the rest of us.

Let 's read from Rennyo Shonin's *Gobunsho*.

> *In silently contemplating the transient nature of human existence,*
> *nothing is more fragile and fleeting in this world than the life of man.*
> *Thus, we have not heard of human life lasting for 10,000 years. Life*
> *passes swiftly, and who among men can maintain his form for even a*
> *hundred years? Whether I go before others, whether others go before*
> *me, whether it be today or tomorrow, who is to know? Those who depart*
> *before us are as countless as the drops of dew. Though in the morning we*
> *may have radiant health, in the evening we may return to white ashes.*
>
> *When the winds of impermanence blow, our eyes are closed forever, and*
> *when the last breath leaves us, our face loses its colour. Though loved*
> *ones gather and lament, everything is to no avail. The body vanishes*
> *from this world with the smoke of creation, leaving only the white ashes.*
>
> *Nothing is more real than this truth of life. The fragile nature of human*
> *existence underlies both the young and the old; therefore we must, one*
> *and all, turn to the teachings of the Buddha, and awaken to the ultimate*
> *source of life. By so understanding the meaning of death, we come to*
> *appreciate the meaning of life that is to be treasured, because it is unre-*
> *peatable. By virtue of true compassion, let us realise the unexcelled*
> *value of this existence, let us live together with gratitude in our heart.*

We don't know what is happening to Bill, but he's returned to white ashes.
He was a follower of the Lord Buddha. Perhaps at this moment he waits
outside the Nirvana gates. I knew and respected him. Let's send our good
wishes whatever religious faith we have or none. Let's end this funeral
service in silence, finishing with the sound of the bell.'

Like Bill's life, one moment the funeral was rolling along and then it was over.
The music and chanting faded away. The large Japanese meditation bell tinkled
three times, followed by deep silence. I waited outside in fine drizzle to shake
hands with each mourner as they went. One skeletal young man covered in
tattoos, even on his bald head, shouted: 'Nice one Rev' before climbing onto a
damp motor bike. I went home by car – moved and empty. I was too full emotionally. Some deep mysteries had been touched in this ceremony. I was part of
some huge process, tapping into the flow of a great river. Just for a single
moment we had felt the original nature of that old rogue Bill.

Chapter 8
Nothing Special

The greatest achievement seems like falling short,
but its effects are beyond measure.
Being filled up feels like being emptied out,
But never like running dry.
Straightforwardness seems obscure.
Great skill seems clumsy.
Great intelligence looks foolish.
Great eloquence sounds like blathering.

(Freke, 1995, p. 87)

A number of years ago I ran a workshop on 'Gentle Teaching' for the Irish Association of Psychologists in the lovely county of Galway. At the finish a close friend asked one eminent colleague what he'd thought of it. After some considerable thought he responded: 'I enjoyed it but there wasn't anything new'. He wanted to be surprised, to learn some fresh techniques. He wanted to be filled rather than emptied. We are obsessed with the quest for the fresh and fashionable, when we need reminding of what we've already forgotten. The desire for newness has become a serious obstacle to seeing ordinary miracles, no longer appreciated by jaded eyes.

We don't see the world fully or properly any more. We don't have the vital energy running right through us, like young children in a playgroup with their noise and bustle. Every single moment, those energetic chimps uncover something fresh in the hardly noticed – by adults anyway – sticks and stones of the playground. My Mam said that when very young I made steam trains from old shoeboxes and pushed them ceaselessly around the narrow hallway. We recall things rather than see them ever afresh. My father-in-law used to injure himself every year or so. Whilst he was working in London, his wife would radically rearrange the furniture. He'd come back on the train, enter the bedroom and leap on the bed, except it wasn't there. It was across the other side of the room. The picture in his mind's eye didn't exist out there anymore.

We struggle with the great differences between our imagination and what exists. There were once two students, both extremely proud of their teacher. They wished many others to appreciate him. A great opportunity arose for publicity. A new temple had been opened and respected teachers traditionally scribed their teachings on the fresh walls. At their request, the temple authorities gave permission for their guru to write an important message. Nervously they asked the great man if he'd write something. He agreed enthusiastically.

They waited anxiously outside. The guru was in and out in a moment. Inside they saw the single miserly Chinese character for 'ATTENTION' on the far wall. It was very unimpressive, unlikely to attract any prospective students. They wondered how to raise this problem and eventually arrived at a solution.

'Master. Your message is a little short' He responded quickly: 'Why didn't you say?' He went into the temple again and exited almost as quickly as the first time. They rushed in to see. Now the message on the temple wall was much longer. It read: 'ATTENTION. ATTENTION. ATTENTION. ATTENTION.' Nothing complicated or flashy, certainly nothing fresh, but if they couldn't see the vital importance of mindful practice they didn't deserve such a great and persistent teacher.

Stupidity
Montaigne (1958, p. 287) noted:

> *'Stupidity is a bad quality; but to be unable to bear it, to be vexed and fretted by it, as is the case with me, is another kind of disease that is hardly less troublesome, and of this I am now going to accuse myself.'*

It is so easy to become chronically self-righteous and stupid. When you're naturally dogmatic like me, it is very easy. Like Montaigne, I have a gift for bearing it with bad grace. I constantly struggle with the feeling that life is teaching me the wrong lessons; that I know best what I should be learning.

Humility is an uncommon human quality and spirituality can become an effective cover for all sorts of arrogance. 'I'm more holistic than thou' is best avoided. We do need to take things apart, to ask shrewder questions – but also to avoid the pitfalls of self-cherishing and missing the whole picture. The Tao trail points to essential unity. This is definitely not some unattainable Holy Grail but an ever-present reality that we stumble over but rarely recognise. It is a practice done amid the washing of clothes, using the vacuum cleaner and cleaning dirty saucepans. The healing takes place from where we are, not from where we might like to be. We turn away from trying to better ourselves and become what we already are.

The basis of all healing lies in being a vehicle for vital energy. Nothing special. This asks that we are gentler with ourselves and with others;

learning to accept ourselves; that we recognise in our hearts the essential connectedness; surrendering our different images of perfection as deluded measures of the world and seeing it with reverence, honesty and love. As Sawaki Roshi commented: 'Everybody is in his own dream. The discrepancies that exist between the dreams are the problem' (Uchiyama, 1990, p. 75)

I've supported my disabled friend Kavan for more than two years now. We met him earlier when I was struggling with the microwave oven in his tiny flat. He's been a great teacher to me. I've learned lots that I definitely didn't want to learn, the heart of real spiritual learning. I've had to come down from the high mountain of all my books and academic research and genuinely experience the front-line – actually working with disabled people rather than simply writing about it, much more challenging.

Kavan and I have very different dreams and scripts but they are almost certainly from the same play. In our heads, things are supposed to run smoothly and coherently, but they rarely do. He helps me to experience more fully the frustrations that emerge from the huge gap between 'supposed to' and actual life, and how and why we are both bewildered and disappointed by life's constant 'imperfections'. Like him, I'm usually seeking more control; wanting the world to be more as I imagined it to be. We are both profoundly disappointed with the world as it is, that it constantly fails to live up to our reasonable expectations.

As we grow older, we both learn to live more comfortably with our everyday stupidities, rather than get any wiser. I get older rather than wiser. I experience my daily existence as continually tripping over the obvious, being mind-bogglingly insensitive and stubborn, and retaining an impassioned resistance to any major learning. In the past, I had a great tendency to hit myself really hard when falling from some presumed high standards. A great rage of disappointment would make my throat sore. Nowadays that happens rather less; not the attainment of any wisdom, just getting fatigued. Like Montaigne, I've grown a little more comfortable with the stupidity both in myself and in others. It feels more and more like a pair of old slippers.

Beginner's Mind
This kind of stupidity arises because we lose our essential 'beginner's mind'. This does not involve some high standard to be attained or some subtle spiritual achievement. Beware of making it yet another examination. Dogen Zenjii expressed it well: 'Each evening we die, each morning we are born

again.' If that really happens to us, we can bring freshness to each dawn, but mostly we cannot. Instead I carry the heavy stones of each previous day on my ever aching back – all those worries and concerns from the previous day, weeks or even years; still lying there, making it difficult to dance and even to sleep. Stones and rocks of guilt, blame, injury, sorrow, mourning – I'm sighing deeply whilst writing them down such an endless list. I rarely seem to shed anything, just add this heavy burden over the long years.

Bion, a pioneering group psychotherapist, expressed a sense of this after confiding his anxieties to a new group.

> *I soon find that my confidence is not very well received. Indeed, there is some indignation that I should express such feelings without seeming to appreciate that this group is entitled to expect something from me. I do not dispute this, but content myself with pointing out clearly that the group cannot be getting from me what they feel they are entitled to expect. I wonder what these expectations are, and what has aroused them.* (Bion, 1961, p. 30)

Once when starting some group training for Centrepoint, a London-based agency for the homeless, I was attacked by several group members because I remained silent whilst they expressed a number of overwhelming (to me anyway) expectations.

As we've noted previously, beginner's mind is different from ignorance. Bion had read widely on group therapy and had had some previous experience but wished not to get in the way of direct experience and started each new group afresh. Observing students over many years, I have noticed that their semidigested reading often obstructs the communication process. At worst the client feels as though he or she has been vomited over. The embryonic professionals are seeking significances and patterns that were in the books but not necessarily in the present experience.

Zen Master Dogen was given a salutary lesson in significance by a Chinese *tenzo*, the head cook of a monastery. In the thirteenth century, Dogen made a dangerous sea journey from Japan to China, surviving typhoons and pirates. After his arrival he met the *tenzo*, who had walked miles to buy shitake mushrooms – brought by the boat from Japan – to flavour the monastery's noodle soup. Dogen was ready to sell him the mushrooms he'd brought, but so impressed was he with the old cook that he invited him to stay the night and have a meal. The *tenzo* declined, saying he had to return that same evening.

'But surely there are other monks who could prepare the meal in your absence?' 'I have been put in charge of this work. How can I leave it to others?' responded the cook.

'But why does a venerable elder such as yourself waste time doing the hard work of a head cook. Why don't you spend your time practising meditation or studying the words of the masters?' The *tenzo* burst out laughing. 'My dear foreign friend, it's clear that you don't understand what Zen practice is all about. When you have time please visit me at the monastery so we can discuss these matters more fully.' Dogen had obviously never read the *Tao Te Ching*: 'Cooking a small fish and ruling a big country, need equal care'. (Freke, 1995, p. 104)

Dogen eventually visited this fine cook and the marvellous book *Tenzo Kyokun* ('Instructions for the Zen Cook') was one result. (Wright, 1983) It has been an inspiration over many long years, although I'm no great fan of Dogen – a bit too much like St Paul rather than Jesus for my taste. But the *tenzo's* marvellous advice is to cook with what we have already: the herbs, the rice, the noodles and all our own skills and difficulties are in the cupboard – there is no need for any others.

Homelessness and violence have been my lifelong herbs, to use with wisdom and discipline, but only in brief flashes. Nothing is more important or more sacred than these tasks given to us, whatever we are doing at this very moment. Our anger, impatience, stupidity, love and perseverance all flavour the delicious soup, along with Dogen's shitake mushrooms, which we can now buy in the supermarket. I'm not sure what I learned from being homeless and suffering violence, and later from being a psychiatric patient. I know something of my stupidity in that I write and talk too much and hardly ever listen. My long dead Mam said: 'Our David only ever listens to the things he wants to hear.'

We do need a beginner's mind, that strips away our fixed notions and dogmas. 'You can't go in with preconceived ideas of how to "fix up" the situation. You have to ask [homeless] people what they need and empower them to find their own solutions' (Glassman and Fields, 1996, p. 91). The hard part of any genuine learning is to give up the ideas you already have, much harder than acquiring new ones. I refused to go to the last homeless planning seminar in the city where I live. We have a big and probably increasing homeless problem in Cambridge. The city council has developed a fresh overall strategy for dealing with it. It is a clever plan, very much like the half-a-dozen other plans I've seen over the last 30 years. It is an excellent example of top-down planning. No homeless people were formally invited to this crucial seminar. The planners had precious ideologies that would have been swirled away by the direct experience of homeless people.

> *In Japan we have the phrase **shoshin,** which means 'beginner's mind'.*
> *The goal of practice is always to keep our beginner's mind. Suppose*
> *you recite the Prajna Paramita Sutra only once. It might be a very*
> *good recitation. But what would happen to you if you recited it twice,*
> *three times, four times or more? You might easily lose your original*
> *attitude towards it. The same thing will happen in your other Zen*
> *practices. For a while you will keep your beginner's mind, but if you*
> *continue to practice one, two, three years or more, although you may*
> *improve some, you are liable to lose the limitless meaning of original*
> *mind.* (Suzuki, 1973, p. 21)

How can we possibly maintain that freshness and vitality in the things we do everyday?

I am a stupid and complaining Zen monk, a great trouble to everyone, who has learnt hardly anything from the finest teachers, largely wasting their time. But there are one or two brief moments, when *even* I understand the long dead Chinese *tenzo's* message. We are not asked to become better persons, to be improved models – thank goodness. All that arrant nonsense is a further expression of disastrous craving, intense human suffering, deep discontent and splitting. The Lord Buddha leads us boldly to be what and where we are. If we follow him we can uncover our true and original nature. Some of us are lions, yet many others are dandelions – we develop and blossom just as we are, without pretending to be anything else, better or worse than we truly are.

This is the meaning of the Tao without meaning.

> *The secret of the way proposed by Chuang Tzu is therefore not the accu-*
> *mulation of virtue and merit proposed by Ju, but **wu wei,** the non-doing,*
> *or non-action, which is not intent upon results and is not concerned with*
> *consciously laid plans or deliberately organized endeavours: 'My*
> *greatest happiness consists precisely in doing nothing whatever that is*
> *calculated to obtain happiness ... Perfect joy is to be without joy.*
> (Merton, 1965, p. 24)

We are happiest when unconcerned and not knowing whether we are happy or not. The more carefully we fire the arrow from the bow, the more likely we will miss the target.

Living in the Moment
Giving complete attention to someone in distress is difficult. The mind plays many tricks with past and future, moving chaotically between different times and experiences. Enright writes:

> *I am quite serious in asserting that most of us in the mental health pro-*
> *fessions, are much of the time, to a surprising extent, not fully aware of*
> *our actual present. Much of the content of our consciousness is remem-*
> *bering, speculating, planning, . . . or carrying on a busy inner dialogue.*
> *More specifically we professionals, sitting with a patient may be diag-*
> *nosing, 'prognosing', planning our next intervention, wondering what*
> *time it's getting to be, etc. – we are only rarely being really open to our*
> *experience of self and other . . . . Engaged as we are with our own*
> *phantoms, we attend only sketchily to the other. Since he then seems*
> *rather pale and incomplete, we fill him our with our own projections*
> *and react vigorously to these* (Enright, in Rowan, 1983, p. 47).

I was reflecting on being really listened to, being profoundly heard. It has happened so few times and only for brief moments, usually in the formal presence of Zen teachers. Each experience was deeply intense and wholesome. Each time I felt both naked and relieved. I was seen for who I was, rather than who or what I might become. I was accepted just I was – warts and all. The social games and strategies I used were no longer necessary.

Two Zen monks set out for a monastery some distance away. On the journey they came to a river, swollen by unseasonal mountain rains. A young woman in formal dress was waiting, unable to cross by herself. The older monk picked her up and carried her through the waters. The monks walked on for ten miles in silence, but when they came into sight of their monastery the younger monk asked: 'Why did you break the vows of our Order and have physical contact with that woman?' The older monk replied: 'I put that woman down ten miles back. I see you're still carrying her'.

So there were all these monastic rules, regulations and even vows. Perhaps the older monk had broken one of them but in the name of compassion rather than lust. The young woman couldn't cross the river without help. But the younger monk couldn't lay the event down. Throughout the long mountainous walk he worried, and asked for clarification with a hint of rebuke: 'Why did you break your vows?' He carried that woman deep inside his head, unable to live in the moment, unable to enjoy the breeze and the countryside, constantly reflecting on broken vows, guilt and fears.

A poor man came to the Archbishop Esai and pleaded: 'My family is so destitute that we have had nothing to eat for several days. My wife and children are about to die of starvation. Please have compassion'. At the time there was no clothing, food, or other possessions in the temple but Esai saw a thin piece of copper allocated to make a halo for a Buddha statue. He took it and broke it up, giving the man a piece, telling him to exchange it for food.

The disciples reproached Esai. 'That is nothing other than the halo for the statue of the Buddha. Is it not a sin to use the Buddha's property for personal use?' Esai responded: 'Yes, it is. Yet think of the Buddhas' will. The Buddha cut off his flesh and limbs and offered them to living human beings. Even if we gave the whole body of the Buddha to the people who are actually about to die of starvation, such an action would certainly be in accordance with the Buddha's will. Even if I fall into hell because of this sin, I have just saved living beings from starvation'. (Dogen, 1987, pp. 68–9)

These students had lost the plot. The sacred halo was needed to feed a destitute family that day, not for formal worship.

Jesus allowed the hungry disciples to pick corn on the Sabbath and was severely criticised by Pharisees. They stared at the finger, not at the moon. Jesus responded: 'The Sabbath was made for Man, not Man for the Sabbath' The purpose of making statues was to serve those pilgrims following the pathway of the Buddha. 'To save all sentient beings.' Following the Buddha, living in the Tao, is a daily discipline of infinite subtlety, not some crude motorcycle handbook to be followed diagram by diagram.

We can easily turn a vow from a joyous aspiration into an instrument for the severest self-punishment, a form of Buddhist Puritanism:

we turn it against ourselves in an inverted arrogance. We can use it as proof of our worthlessness and weakness if we even think about breaking it. Rather than allowing our promise to be something that helps us and lifts us up, we use it to beat ourselves down. But when we are depressed, we need our vow more than at any other time. We can use it to help our healing, to make decisions easier, and sometimes even to keep us safe and alive.(Martin, 1999, p. 141)

My life has been full of such oppressive feelings, taking me right away from living in the present time.

Chogyam Trungpa wrote:

The essence of meditation is nowness. Whatever one tries to practice is not aimed at achieving a higher state or at following some theory or idea, but simply, without any object or ambition, trying to see what is here and now. One has to become aware of the present moment . . .'
(Trungpa, 1969)

That is so very easy to write but so very hard to practice, especially in ordinary, everyday life, full of the fires of desire. I've sat for so many years on a black zen cushion, my mind running rampantly all over the place although the body was still. In the beginning I had clear ideas about the point and purpose of meditation. I was going to be enlightened, to become illuminated, to be a better person, to listen more carefully . . . The list was very long.

My favourite cartoon contains some of that stupidity. Two huge hippos are standing in a swamp, stretching away into the distance, infinite and featureless. One comments to the other: 'Do you know I keep thinking it's Thursday'. Well I spend a great deal of time, wondering whether it's a Thursday or how many shopping days there are to Christmas.

As the years rolled on – five, ten, twenty years of meditation – most of these ideas slipped away. They became increasingly irrelevant. I remained the same undisciplined slob but the many ambitions and the register of supposed achievements fell away. I wasn't making any genuine progress but cared less. I dropped those ideas. They slipped off my back, usually without me noticing. I had fewer and fewer ideas about why I did this or that. I didn't know any more what the point was. I just sat for most of the time, as the hours rolled interminably on. I felt settled.

Ordinary
Everyday bustle, hustle, razzmatazz and greed is a far cry from Zen Master Unmon: 'If you walk, just walk. If you sit, just sit; but don't wabble, whatever you do'. (Blyth, 1960, p. 116) Unmon takes us right back to the eternal Tao. Just to be our ordinary selves; living with simple and necessary

rituals and activities; unconcerned with the complex social games played inside and outside. What does it matter what people believe and expect? Is it practicable to live in that way any more? Can we avoid reflecting on what we see in others and guessing what they feel and think so we can calculate . . . ? After opening Pandora's Box, can we ever go back? YES. It doesn't mean complacency and self-satisfaction. It means the difference between joyful service and covert spiritual greed.

Of course there is an inherent and healthy drive deep within us, to create a better and more natural state, to live more simply, to be less plastic and conformist, free of the self- created internal noise and chatter. But even this drive can become an exploited trap – a spiritual materialism, a sophisticated variation on greed. We can be immensely greedy for possessions of the spiritual kind, to be liberated, awakened, to walk on water. We can build superior pyramids of ideologies. We can develop photographs of loaves of bread rather than bake the delicious and nourishing loaves themselves.

I recall two crucial things about a spiritual quest many years ago to the important Catholic shrine of Medjegorje in Bosnia. I remember the long haul up the stony hill to where the teenage visionaries had seen the Virgin Mary, and the quiet compassion with which everyone helped each other, even though they were mostly bewildered strangers. I recall that the cafés sold the most expensive cheese sandwiches ever. Somehow the two went together – the sacred and the profane, the spiritual and the materialistic. These are two very different ways of profiting.

The novelist Joseph Conrad's tombstone bears a quotation from a sixteenth-century poem by Edmund Spenser that he greatly loved:

> *Sleep after Toyle,*
> *Port after stormie Seas,*
> *Ease After Warre,*
> *Death After Life Does Greatly Please*

Spenser reminds us of the essential realities of human life and death. Conrad knew well of the mariner's life that strips away the triviality of those trends that currently suffocate us. We need to return to some quiet and authentic traditions. They stress everyday living and relationships rather than anything wonderful and extraordinary. Our search for magical and superior techniques is not only unnecessary but also part of our sickness. We should be deeply suspicious of those forces, spiritual and therapeutic, that offer the possibility of major change, purchased through increased power and money.

Bankei answered a question put by a lay student:

> *Everyone says that you're able to read others' minds. Is it true?'*
> *Bankei responded: 'There's no place in my school for strange things*
> *like that. Even if I did have such an ability, because of the unborn-ness*
> *of the Buddha mind, I wouldn't use it. People get the idea that I can*
> *read minds from hearing me comment on the concerns of those who*
> *come to see me. I can't read minds. I'm no different from any of you.*
> *When you dwell in the Buddha-mind, which is the very source of all the*
> *Buddhas' supernatural powers, everything is resolved and in perfect*
> *harmony without recourse to such powers. So I don't need to get*
> *involved in such side issues. All the true unborn Dharma needs to do*
> *the job is direct personal comments on you and your lives.* (Waddell,
> 1984, p. 69)

Bankei rightly turns his back on this suggestion of trashy magic and gimmicks. He had no need for such tricks to live his life and to help. He didn't need to read minds or know the souls of men. He was an ordinary man, not seeking to be different, special or superior. He was no different in skills and talents from any other person, laying no claim to special insights, unlike many contemporary counsellors. He simply avoided being distracted and learned to prevent his mind from breaking into thousands of tiny fragments. He was immensely earthy and pragmatic, rooted in the soil of ordinary living.

As he commented:

> *There was once a monk in my temple who had been dozing off. Another*
> *monk saw him and really laid into him with a stick. I reprimanded him:*
> *'Why hit him when he's enjoying a pleasant nap? Do you think he*
> *leaves the Buddha mind and goes somewhere else when he sleeps?'*
> *Now I don't urge people to sleep around here. But once they are*
> *asleep, you're making a serious mistake if you hit them . . . If you stay*
> *awake, you stay awake. If you sleep, you sleep. When you sleep, you*
> *sleep in the same Buddha-mind you were awake in. When you're*
> *awake, you're awake in the same Buddha-mind you were sleeping in.*
> (ibid, p. 50)

This is the damned trouble with inspirational spiritual teaching by great teachers such as Bankei. It sounds so ordinary – no great drum rolls or cymbals. You only realise you've had it when it's too late. Blink or yawn and you've missed it. It all seems so banal at the time. You were expecting lightning to flash and thunder to roll and there's only a slight cough or a shake of the hand. You were looking up in the air to find the stars and planets and it came silently on the back of a blowing leaf.

There's an old Chinese story about a man who heard of a great teacher, many hundreds of miles away. He walked over seven mountain ranges; across ten broad rivers and countless streams; was robbed twice; hungered and thirsted many times; wore out half a dozen pairs of stout shoes. Eventually, after nearly a year, he arrived exhausted but content at the remote place where this great teacher was living and teaching. At the first meeting, he prostrated himself three times in the dust, as was the custom, and begged to be taught. 'Please teach me, Oh Great One. I have come from afar.' The Great One responded brusquely – 'Do good and avoid evil', and then silence.

After a long wait the deeply disappointed student replied: 'Is that it? Is that all? Is this teaching the reason why I sold everything, crossed all those rivers, nearly died in the mountains, walked a thousand miles, was robbed of all my possessions – to hear what every five-year-old child knows already?' 'Ah', said the Great One, 'a five year old child may know it but an eighty-year-old man can't practice it.'

You can sympathise with the exhausted student. He was expecting a drum roll at the least, some really clever comments of mystifying complexity; the communication of secret tantric empowerments. He'd made a massive journey at great personal cost and yet travelled no distance at all – his head still firmly in the clouds, clogs covered by unseen dogshit. He'd suffered, made very considerable sacrifices and expected some tangible reward.

The moving of the legs one in front of the other, and the ideas of liberation whirling about inside the head are easy. Spin-dryer mind. Everyday and banal practice is infinitely hard, as the Great One explained to the tired and angry student. If he had any sense the student would have stayed with his new-found teacher and studied hard to find a basis for solid living. However my best guess is that he left almost immediately and found someone with much better tricks and a more sophisticated spiel. That would have been his great loss.

Dragons and Tigers
Most of us are haunted by an eternal succession of demons and dragons, every bit as vivid as scenes in the great Saxon epic *Beowulf*. Most of us spend some time on the run, attempting to escape the modern equivalent of those horrors. Among the homeless are many emotional 'runners' – people trying vainly to escape ordinary living. Everyday Taoist practice is about learning to face the dragons and tigers – gently and slowly.

There is an old story about dragons and a temple. Paintings of dragons are a feature of great power in new temples. Many centuries ago an abbot from central China was visiting a colleague in the far south. The occasion was the opening of a new temple, and seeing the traditional dragon painting for the first time, the abbot was very impressed with its power and energy. He asked his colleague whether the man might be interested in working at his new temple. The colleague introduced him to the painter so that arrangements might be made directly.

The exchange was very agreeable and it was arranged for the artist to travel up in a month or two to execute the commission. The two men shook hands and as they parted, the abbot asked: 'You have seen a real dragon. You do paint from real life?' The artist was shocked. 'I didn't know there were any real dragons'. The abbot said firmly that dragons lived close to his temple and under no circumstances would he ever employ a painter who just used his imagination. Somewhat ashamed the immensely curious painter said: 'What if I come up early, see the dragons and then do the painting?' This was acceptable.

So a few weeks later the painter made the long journey northwards and arrived towards nightfall. The following morning the abbot took him far out into the thick bush where the dragons lived. He left the unwilling artist on his own in a small clearing with water and bread. 'I will be back in three days to collect you. Sit very still because these dragons are easily spooked'. The artist was a city boy and soon became nervous. He sat right through the cold days and nights, but saw nothing and heard little.

On the fourth morning the abbot arrived. 'Well. What did you see?' The depressed painter said: 'Nothing. I'm cold and frozen. I want to go home'. The abbot asked: 'Did you move at all?' 'Well of course I moved,' said the artist angrily. 'Ah' said the abbot, 'that'll be it. These dragons are highly nervous. But you can't give up now. Think of painting dragons from real life instead of just from your imagination'. The guilty victim was persuaded to spend another three days and nights with some more bread and water.

On the seventh morning the abbot returned. Before he could speak the furious painter screamed: 'I'm so furious, cold and frustrated. I've spent six long days and nights in this desperately forsaken spot and seen absolutely nothing'. His face went scarlet and his body shook violently. The abbot waited until silence was restored: 'Now you've really seen the dragon, come back to the temple and paint it'. Even today, people say that the dragon in this remote temple is so powerful because it was painted from real life.

This next story was told to me in China many years ago at the place where the supposed events had taken place a thousand years or more before – the tigers cave. The old abbot in charge of a monastery wanted to retire but had two possible Dharma heirs. One was young and nervous; the other was older and very muscular. He announced to both that he would retire in a few days and go to live with his sister. One of them would be the new abbot. They'd undergo a test and the winner would replace him. They had to go on different evenings to the tiger's cave about ten miles away and stay the whole night.

The muscular monk arrived at the cave at dusk. He sat firmly on a rock with his black robes wrapped round him against the cold. He concentrated on his meditation. Halfway between dusk and dawn he discovered why it was called the tiger's cave. Something large was moving through the bushes. He reconcentrated his efforts and it passed close by. In the morning, he got up very stiffly and walked back to the monastery.

The nervous monk arrived at dusk the next evening. He tried to get comfortable, but the evening was cold and the rock very hard. He shifted about a lot. Half way between dusk and dawn he made the same discovery as his predecessor. Something large was moving slowly. He waited tensely until it was about three leaps away and then darted for the nearest tree, climbing speedily upwards. He stayed there until dawn, when he climbed down and returned to the monastery.

The abbot listened to both accounts. He sat silently for a short period. Then he called for his assistant and pointed at the nervous monk. 'Take him and shave his head and prepare him for the formal ceremony, the handing over of the bowls and robes'. When they had gone, the muscular monk could hardly restrain himself. 'I passed the test and he did not. He got frightened and climbed a tree.' His face was scarlet with fury and injustice.

The abbot replied quietly: 'My son – you are brave beyond all imagination. But the one essential quality of a successful abbot is that he should be alive. A dead abbot is no good to a monastery. How long do you think you would stay alive, sitting so still while a hungry tiger passed close by?' So in the contest between the hare and the tortoise, the samurai and the neurotic, the latter wins. No great leaps are necessary, just the Tao of simple survival.

Uchiyama Roshi wrote:

> *when you climb a mountain, you climb moment by moment, one step at a time. It's not that you climb a mountain only when you reach the summit. To advance one step at a time is what's important. We live moment by moment, step by step. This is an activity of the whole universe. It is an activity that is good for nothing . . . . There is nothing to pick up or throw away. There is no where to go . . . . With this pure life force within myself, I live always here and now, manifesting the whole universe. (Uchiyama, 1990, p. 124)*

We're not asked to jump over high buildings, wrestle with tigers, turn pebbles into gold or even to lead a reasonably good life, whatever that might mean. We are asked to be simply human. What that really means for each of us is uncovered during our life-long pilgrimage. It is a journey through fog and mist, fear and anger; through stupidity and some very occasional flashes of wisdom. Montaigne (1958, p. 396) notes:

> *When I dance, I dance; when sleep, I sleep: Yes, and when I am walking with myself in a beautiful orchard, even if my thoughts dwell for a part of the time on distant events, I bring them back for another part of the walk, the orchard, the charm of this solitude, and to myself.*

If only I was capable of that.

Nothing at all special, just very ordinary – living directly in the unfolding moment, whether with tigers or dragons. But is there any greater challenge? It is very simple but not at all easy; difficult to remain undistracted, to avoid life's almost irresistible seductions. This ordinary pilgrimage gradually reveals our true nature and helps our service to others to become a little more joyful. We gradually discover ways to fit in with the infinite world that surrounds us. We uncover some harmonies, a little realisation as with Bion and Feynman – of how very partial our understanding is and how infinite our ignorance. And when in danger we can always climb the nearest tree.

References

Adams, Peter (1999) *The Soul of Medicine – an anthology of illness and healing* London, Penguin

Aitken, Robert (1984) *The Mind of Clover* Hawaii, North Point Press

Alvarez, A (1974) *The Savage God – a study of suicide* London, Penguin

Barclay Report (1982) *Social Workers: their roles and tasks* London, Bedford Square Press

Barker, Pat (1998) *Another World* London, Viking

Barrows, Anita (1995) 'The Ecological Self in Childhood' *Ecopsychology newsletter*, no. 4 (Fall)

Berger, Peter (1977) *Pyramids of Sacrifice* Peter Ludwig

Bion, W R (1961) *Experiences in Groups and other Papers* London, Tavistock

Blake, W (1794) *On Anothers Sorrow: Songs of Innocence*

Blyth, R H (1960) *Zen in English Literature* London, Dutton

Brandon, D (1985a) *Simply Meditate* Preston, Tao

Brandon, D (1985b) *Beginning Zen* Preston, Tao

Brandon, D (1990) *Zen in the Art of Helping* London, Penguin

Brandon, D (1997) *The Trick of Being Ordinary* Cambridge, Anglia Polytechnic University

Brandon, D and Atherton, K (1997) *A Brief History of Social Work* Cambridge, Anglia Polytechnic University

Brandon, D (1997b) 'A Cry for a lost Childhood', *The Guardian* 11 August,

Brandon, D and Atherton, K (1996) *Care Planning Handbook* London, Positive Publications

Brook, Peter (1972) *The Empty Space* London, Pelican

Capra, Fritz (1988) *Uncommon Wisdom* Century London, Hutchinson

Chaudhuri, Anita (2000) Girl Power *The Guardian*, G2, 29 May

Chung-yuan, Chang (1975) *Creativity and Taoism* New York, Wildwood House

Clare, John (1996) *Selected Poems* London, Bloomsbury

Claxton, Guy (1986) *Beyond Therapy* London, Wisdom

Collee John (1996) 'NHS problems are to do with inequality, not resources' *Observer Life*, 10 March

Conrad, Joseph (1973) *Heart of Darkness* London, Penguin

Cupitt D (1998) *Mysticism after Modernity* London, Blackwell

Darwin, Charles (1964) *On the Origin of Species* facsimile edition, Cambridge, Mass, Harvard University Press

Davies, Martin (1985) *The Essential Social Worker – a guide to positive practice* 2nd edn, London, Community Care

Diamond John (1998) *C – because cowards get cancer too. . .* London, Vermilion

Dineen, Tana (1996) *Manufacturing Victims – what the psychology industry is doing to people* Quebec Canada, Robert Davies Publishers

Dogen, Zenjii (1987) *Shobogenzo-zuimonki* Kyoto, Kyoto-shi, Japan, Soto-Zen centre

Donnison, David (1991) *A Radical Agenda – after the New Right and the Old Left* River Oram Press

Downie, R S (1994) *The Healing Arts* Oxford, Oxford University Press

Eliot, T S (1950) *The Cocktail Party* New York, Harcourt, Brace & Co

Feiffer, Jules (1965) cartoon in *The Village Voice* New York

Freke, Timothy (trans.) (1995) *Lao Tzu's Tao Te Ching* London, Piatkus

Galbraith, John Kenneth (1993) *The Culture of Contentment* London, Penguin

Giles, Herbert A (trans.) (1926) *Chuang-tzu – mystic, moralist and social reformer* Shanghai, Kelly and Walsh

Glassman, B (1998) *Bearing Witness – a Zen Masters Lesson in Making Peace* New York, Bell Tower

Glassman, B and Fields, R (1996) *Instructions to the Cook – a Zen Masters lessons in living a life that matters* Bell Tower

Gleick, James (1992) *Genius – Richard Feynman and modern physics* London, Abacus

Gould, Stephen Jay (1994) *Eight Little Piggies – reflections in natural history* London, Penguin

Gould, Stephen Jay (1996) *Lifes Grandeur* London, Jonathan Cape

Graves, Robert (1955) *Greek Myths* London, Penguin

Grof, S and Grof, C (1986) 'Spiritual Emergency: when personal transformation becomes a crisis' *ReVision* 8(2)

Guardian (1996) leader: 13 April

Guggenbühl-Craig, Adolf (1971) *Power in the Helping Professions* Spring Publications

Gunnell, David (1995) 'Suicide and Unemployment' *British Medical Journal,* 24 July

Halifax, Joan (1982) *Shaman: the Wounded Healer* London, Thames and Hudson

Halifax, Joan (1994) *The Fruitful Darkness – reconnecting with the body of the Earth* New York: Harper/Collins

Hanh Thich, Nhat (1982) *Being Peace* London, Rider

Hardy, Jeremy (2000) 'It beggars belief' *The Guardian*, 11 March

Haskel, Peter (1984) *Bankei Zen – translations from the record of Bankei* New York, Grove Weidenfeld

Hawking, Stephen (1988) *A Brief History of Time – from the Big Bang to black holes* London, Bantam

Heaney Seamus (trans.) (1999) *Beowulf* London, Faber

Herrigel Eugen (1985) *Zen in the Art of Archery* London, Arkana

Hobson, R F (1985) *Forms of Feeling – the heart of psychotherapy* London, Tavistock/Routledge

Hofstadter, Douglas and Dennett, Daniel C (1982) *The Minds I – fantasies and reflections on self and soul* London, Penguin

Hood, Thomas 'I remember' in *The Plea of the Mid-summer Fairies* in David Herbert (1993) 'Ever Green Verse' London, Dent

Ives, C (1992) *Zen Awakening and Society* London, MacMillan

Jamison, K R (1996a) *Touched with Fire – manic depressive illness and the artistic temperament* New York, Simon and Schuster

Jamison, K R (1996b) *An Unquiet Mind – a memoir of moods and madness* Basingstoke, Picador

Kalweit, H (1992) *Shamans, Healers, and Medicine Men* Boston, Mass, Shambala

Keble, J (ed.) (1845) *The Works of that learned and judicious divine, Mr Richard Hooker* 3rd ed, Vol 11I, Oxford, Oxford University Press

Keenan, Brian (1992) *An Evil Cradling* London, Hutchinson

Kenyon, N (1997) 'Can't hum along? Good' *Observer*, 30 November

Kornfield, Jack (1993) *A Path with Heart* London, Bantam

Laing, R D (1967) *The Politics of Experience and the Bird of Paradise* London, Penguin

Langland, William (1959) *Piers the Ploughman* London, Penguin

Larkin, Philip and Thwaite, Anthony (1990 *Collected Poems* London, Faber and Faber

Lau, D C (1963) *Lao Tzus Tao Te Ching* London, Penguin

Levi, Primo (1979) *If this is a Man* London, Penguin

Lin Yutang (1938) *The Importance of Living* London, Heinemann

Ling, Trevor (1976) *The Buddha* London, Pelican

Lomas, P (1987) *The Limits of Interpretation* London, Penguin

Lynn, Richard J (1999) *The Classic of the Way and Virtue – Tao-te ching* New York, Columbia University Press

Macaulay, Thomas (1842) 'Lays of Ancient Rome' in David Herbert (1993) *Ever Green Verse* London, Dent

Martin, Philip (1999) *The Zen Path through Depression* San Francisco, Harper

Mearns, Dave and Thorne, Brian (1988) *Person-centred counselling in Action* London, Sage

Mental Health Foundation (MHE) (1997) *Knowing Our Own Minds* London, MHF

Merton, T (1965) *The Way of Chuang Tzu* London, Unwin

Millar, S (1998) 'New Age Guru was age old hypocrite' *Guardian*, 22 June

Miller, Peter and Rose, Nikolas (1986) *The Power of Psychiatry* London, Polity Press

Milton, John *Paradise Lost* Book ii

Montaigne, Michel de (1958) *Essays* London, Penguin

Moore, Wendy (2000) 'Talking Heads' *Observer*, 21 May

Olshansky, Simon (1972) 'Changing Behaviour through Normalisation' in Wolf Wolfensberger *Normalisation* Toronto, Canada, National Institute on Mental Retardation

Pacitti, D (2000) 'Truth to Tell – interview with Noam Chomsky' *Guardian Education*, 18 April

Peile, Colin (1993) 'Determinism versus Creativity: which way for social work?' *Social Work* (USA) 38:2, pp 127–34

Petrioni, P (1993) 'The Return of the Spirit' in Alan Beattie (ed.) *Health and Well Being – a reader* London, MacMillan and Open University

Picardie, R(1998) *Before I say goodbye* London, Penguin

Pirsig, R (1976) *Zen in the Art of Motorcycle Maintenance* London, Corgi

Polsky, H W and Wozner, Y (1989) *Everyday Miracles – the healing wisdom of Hassidic stories* Northvale, NJ, Aronson

Religious Society of Friends (Quakers) (1960) *Christian Faith and Practice* London, The London Yearly Meeting

Reynolds, D K (1980) *The Quiet Therapies - Japanese pathways to personal growth* Hawaii, Hawaii University Press

Rice, Maureen (2000) 'Emergency Rooms' *Observer Life* 7 May

Richan, Willard C and Mendelsohn, Alan R (1973) *Social Work – the unloved Profession* New York, New Viewpoints

Rilke Rainer, Maria (1954) *Letters to a Young Poet* New York, Norton

Rippere, Vicky and Williams, Ruth (1985) (eds) *Wounded Healers – Mental Health Workers experiences of Depression* Chichester, John Wiley

Roethke, Theodore (1986) *Collected Poems* London, Faber

Roth, Harold D (1999) *Original Tao – inward training and the foundation of Taoist mysticism* Columbia, Columbia University Press

Rowan, John (1983) *The Reality Game – a guide to humanistic counselling and therapy* London, Routledge and Kegan Paul

Save the Children (1996) *Health in the Third World* April

Schloegl, Irmgard (1975) *The Record of Rinzai* Buddhist Society

Schloegl, Irmgard (1977) *The Zen Way* London, Sheldon Press

Schwartz, David (1992) *Crossing the River – creating a conceptual revolution in Community and Disability* New york, Brookline Books

Sen, Amartya (1987) *On Ethics and Economics* Oxford, Blackwell

Shaban, Nabil (1996) 'Without Walls: Supercrips and Rejects' *Channel Four TV*, 9 pm, 9 April

Siporin, M (1985) 'Current social work perspectives on clinical practice' *Clinical Social Work Journal* 13:3

Shah, Idries (1966) *The Exploits of the Incomparable Mulla Nasrudin* London, Jonathan Cape

Smail, D (1993) *The Origins of Unhappiness* London, HarperCollins

Sokal, George and Bricmont, Jean (1999) *Intellectual Impostures* London, Profile Books

Stevenson, C (1996) 'The Tao, social constructionism and psychiatric nursing practice and research' *Journal of Psychiatric and Mental Health Nursing*, 3:4

Suzuki, David (1999) *Sacred Balance – rediscovering our place in nature* London, Bantam

Suzuki Shunryu (1973) *Zen Mind, Beginner's Mind* New York, Weatherhill

Thoreau, Henry D (1960) W*alden, or life in the Woods* London, Signet

Titmuss, Richard (1970) *The Gift Relationship – from human blood to social policy* London, Allen & Unwin

Trevor, M H (trans.) (1969) *The Ox and his Herdsman* Tokyo, Hokuseido Press

Trungpa, Chogyam (1969) *Meditation in Action* London, Stuart and Watkins

Trungpa, Chogyam (1987) *Cutting through Spiritual Materialism* Boston, Mass.Shambhala

Uchiyama, K (1990) *The Zen Teaching of 'Homeless' Kodo* Shimogyio-Ku, Japan Schumucho

Waddell, Norman (ed.) (1984) *The Unborn – the Life and Teaching of Zen Master Bankei – 1622-1693* Hawaii, North Point Press

Walsh, R N (1990) *The Spirit of Shamanism* New York, Tarcher/Putnam

Watts, Alan (1979) *Tao – the Watercourse Way* London, Penguin

Wilber, K (1979) *No Boundary - Eastern and Western Approaches to Personal Growth* New York, Center Publications

Wilber, Ken (1984) *The Sociable God: Towards a new understanding of Religion* Boston, Mass, Shambala

Wilkes, Ruth (1981) *Social Work with Undervalued Groups* London, Tavistock

Wilkinson, R G (1996) *Unhealthy Societies – the afflictions of Inequality* London, Routledge

Wright, Thomas (trans.) (1983) *From a Zen kitchen: Refining your Life* Weatherhill

Young, Gavin (1991) *In Search of Conrad London,* London, Hutchinson

Zohar, Danah & Marshall, Ian (1994) *The Quantum Society* London, Flamingo